The Forward Book of Poetry

2017

FORWARD
Worldwide

LONDON

First published in Great Britain by
Forward Worldwide · 83 Clerkenwell Road · London EC1R 5AR
in association with
Faber & Faber · Bloomsbury House · 74-77 Great Russell Street
London WC1B 3DA

ISBN 978 0 571 33080 5 (paperback)

Compilation copyright © Forward Worldwide 2016
Foreword copyright © Malika Booker 2016

Cover image copyright © Joe Tilson

Printed and bound by CPI Group (UK) · Croydon CRO 4YY

MIX
Paper from
responsible sources
FSC® C016486
www.fsc.org

A CIP catalogue reference for this book
is available at the British Library.

To Lucy Coles, Casey Jones and Will Scott

Contents

Highly Commended Poems 2016

Foreword

This year marks the twenty-fifth birthday of the Forward Prizes, which have grown to be the most prestigious awards for poetry published in Britain and Ireland annually. Their founder, William Sieghart, created the prizes – and this series of companion anthologies – to showcase contemporary poetry to both a literary and non-literary audience. He wanted to promote poetry as a living, breathing art form, one that would continue to attract new readers and, having attracted them, keep them. And his mission has succeeded. Over the years, the prizes have demonstrated an uncanny ability to pick out good new poets, many of whom have gone on to ever greater things. The Forwards are not just part of the landscape; they have shaped that landscape too.

How do they work? There are three categories: Best First Collection, Best Collection and Best Single Poem. Publishing houses and small presses are invited to submit poetry collections, while magazines, journals, and – for the first time this year – e-zines send a selection of individual poems published in 2015-2016. Five judges are chosen to read the poetry and together they shortlist five entries from each category. I was fortunate to chair this year's panel: Man Booker International winner George Szirtes, former Best First Collection winner Liz Berry, the American poet and editor of *Poetry* magazine, Don Share, and the singer-songwriter Tracey Thorn.

Each week our letter boxes rattled, our doorbells rang, we signed for parcels, boxes or bundles of padded envelopes, vacuum-packed with 2016's yield of poetry. We flicked open countless front covers to consume, sigh, cry, laugh, and absorb, as we read and re-read. And as we began, so did the questions. We started to notice a list of criteria growing longer with each book read. What makes a good poem, or poetry collection? Does a collection need a sense of consistency? Should it have a strong beginning that builds? What about formal constraints? Should the poems be 'authentic', whatever that might mean? Maybe they need to be experimental, to push boundaries and clearly demarcate a fresh unique voice. Should each poem in a book be obliged to earn its place? The questions swelled with each collection until we found books that simply broke all of the rules and yet were so original that they would elicit an utterance only poetry seeks of the human heart – the breathy sigh of appreciation, like an extended exhale.

Reading so much is not always comfortable. I write this sitting on a veranda in Treasure Beach, Montego Bay, Jamaica – my backyard is the sea. The scene is tranquil; waves gently caress the seashore. Yet looks deceive. The locals warn us that it is dangerous to swim here: the undertow is so strong that even seasoned swimmers have been known to drown. In the act of writing, I begin to understand that great poems are like this sea: beautiful, sorrowful or plain on first glance, yet with each new encounter revealing intense undercurrents, as they drag the reader into a world at once familiar and strange. I muse on the ways poems, consumed en masse, can drown one's imagination with a multiplicity of sensory and emotional experiences. You need strength, we discovered, to read strong poetry.

When the five of us convened in May in a beautiful book-lined room near Green Park in London, clutching our long lists of favourite candidates, all braced to debate, cajole, argue, convince, deliberate, we learnt to our surprise that most of our lists overlapped. And yet we each arrived there from different starting points.

One of the main aims of these prizes and this anthology is to inspire a love of poetry in a wide range of audiences, and as such Tracey Thorn's presence on the panel was invaluable. A musician who loves poetry – but is not, unlike the rest of the judges, a poet – she reminded us that the non-poet reader is vital in this selection process. Don Share's editorial knowledge provided insightful, careful readings that cut straight to the poems' heartbeats. George Szirtes, with his vast experience as a lecturer, translator and veteran of judging panels, was a repository of poetic wisdom, while Liz Berry applied a fresh and passionate interrogation of each work.

Our judging tasked us to be rigorous, like discerning chefs hired to choose a banquet suitable for many palates, where each dish must remain distinct. The shortlisted poets we chose tackle subjects that include grief, nature and migration. They play with language – or, often, with languages. Some imbue their work with strong northern or Scottish dialects, some are ambitious in the portrayal of war and exile. They travel, they speak in tongues. They each retain strong individual voices.

Every so often one of our national newspapers stirs itself to print an article which somehow asks and answers the question 'Is poetry dead?', as if the idle query itself were still alive. History tells us that poetry is one of our oldest art forms, one that existed across civilisations and definitely, defiantly, reigned orally before the advent of print. Dispel the myths and clichés about poetry by reading – and sharing – the works in this book.

Malika Booker, *June 2016*

Preface

The poems contained in this anthology are all by poets shortlisted
or highly commended for work published in the past 12 months.
They are so fresh from the furnace that they risk burning your mouth.

Certainly, I defy anyone to read, say, the work of Harry Giles
without trying out his mixture of Scots and Orkney on the tongue.
Giles can probably do it better – he is already a celebrated performer
– but your efforts will change the way you hold yourself. You will
become musical, your feet may stamp, eyes bulge, shoulders tense. Your
muttering will turn to shouts and laughter. If you are not careful, you
will draw an audience. You will certainly have a vivid new vocabulary
in which to tell them to go away, or to come closer. You will also
understand something important about contemporary Scotland.

Vivid, new: though perfectly good words, they are too small to
sum up the mature power of the poets of the Best Collection shortlist.
Take Vahni Capildeo, Trinidad-born with an Oxford doctorate in Old
Norse. She deploys her familiarity with Creole, Sanskrit, Old English,
French, Spanish, Latin and the rest so lightly that it's only on looking
up from the page that you realise she has somehow led the reader to
enact the book's subject: making a home in a place that does not always
make you feel welcome. Or as she writes, 'Language is my home, I say,
not one particular language.'

It's a resonant line for these troubled times. It certainly resonates
with Ian Duhig, who marries playfulness and formal skill with a strong
moral drive, using his formidable breadth of literary and non-literary
references – songs, legends, jokes – to lend voice to those voiceless he
has encountered daily in his ongoing work with the homeless in Leeds.
And with the Kurdish poet Choman Hardi – once an asylum seeker in
Britain, now a professor of English Literature in Iraqi Kurdistan – whose
words illuminate the darkest of places.

There is no one-size-fits-all vocabulary that can suit so many
different poets, but – to continue with the Best Collection shortlistees
– Alice Oswald and Denise Riley, both hugely admired prize-winning
writers, use their acute awareness of language to push it to very personal
limits. In Oswald's case, this means searching to capture that which
lies always just beyond our apprehension – the forces of nature and

history in the silence between a blackbird's notes, say – while Riley, precise always, hammers words into new expressions for the deadly commonplace of bereavement.

What we think of as English is growing all the time, and each of these poets is on the frontline of change, contributing strong powers of observation and expression to the endless re-drafting of the language. Why is this so important? Because it's needed, now, more than ever. (I write in the dismaying days following the 23 June Brexit vote.) In our classrooms there are more than a million children who speak languages in addition to English. Given that selections from Forward books of poetry are now taught in schools, it feels right that the polyglot proficiency of so many young readers will find an answering echo in the poets they study: these poetry choices will feed into ideas of the contemporary and future canon.

The word 'diverse', like the words 'multi-cultural' and 'inclusive', is worn thin by overuse, but all three will inevitably crop up in response to the changes that have come over 25 years to these Forward books and the Forward Prizes. Note that the poets in this book have earned their place because their work makes them central to an ongoing tradition of English literature, not because they are 'marginalised' or 'representative'. They are thoroughly unrepresentative of anything but themselves, endowed with disproportionate talent.

Thanks are due to this year's judges, who are many-cultured, not simply multi-cultural. Their backgrounds feature Hungary, Guyana and Chicago, as well as Hertfordshire and the Black Country. The panel includes a musician, Tracey Thorn; a writer, poet, theatre-maker, Malika Booker; and a poet who trained as an artist, George Szirtes. Don Share, who edits *Poetry* magazine for Chicago's celebrated Poetry Foundation, brings an encyclopaedic knowledge of the current American scene. Liz Berry, a recent winner of the Forward Best First Collection prize, reads and questions with the hungry eye of youth. Between them they have brought new ways of making sense of the world to the judging process.

I also thank Joe Tilson, the artist responsible for this year's beautiful cover design, and his gallery, the Marlborough. Maisie Lawrence, who has this year moved on to a new job after running every aspect of the Forward Prizes administration, knew him to be a poetry lover and invited him to support us: the book's beauty is a tribute to her power to charm.

Thank you, too, to the Forward Worldwide team, especially Casey Jones, Will Scott and Chris Carus. We cannot think of any other literary prize or publication that can count on such unstinting and consistent support – and are profoundly grateful.

Felix Dennis, who for years sponsored the Best First Collection prize, has continued to support us posthumously: we thank Ian Leggett for helping us keep the Dennis legacy alive in words as well as woods. Arts Council England, the Monument Trust, the Esmée Fairbairn Foundation and the Rothschild Foundation all make our work – which includes National Poetry Day as well as the Forward Prizes – possible.

Our trustees – Nigel Bennett, Joanna Mackle, Robyn Marsack, Jacob Sam-La Rose, Giles Spackman and Martin Thomas – have driven us on to ever higher ambitions.

Nick Laurence and Tim Wong of Howoco have worked wonders with our website. Fiona McMorrough, Annabel Robinson and Christopher Bone of FMcM have risen with gusto to the challenge of promoting poetry and poets. Rachel Piercey brought a poet's passion for precision to the proofreading, while the wit and enthusiasm of her fellow poet Joey Connolly informs the biographies.

Finally, thank you to the staff of the Forward Arts Foundation – Peter Cummings and Holly Hopkins – and to its tireless executive director, Susannah Herbert.

William Sieghart, *June 2016*

Shortlisted Poems
The Forward Prize for Best Collection

Vahni Capildeo

Investigation of Past Shoes

INSIDE THE GATEWAY: 1970S RED CLOGS WITH SIDE BUCKLE

The forever shoe, which points homewards, belongs to my mother. When our house was being built, she stepped onto the driveway while the tarmac was still wet, still setting. Ever since that step, the driveway, which slants upwards, bears an imprint of her 1971 footwear. Her footprint says, *Climb! Come with me.* Whoever steps into that impression becomes, for a moment, the leggy wearer of a fire-red clog with a piratical silver buckle on the side.

OUTSIDE THE TEMPLE: GOLD AND SILVER SANDALS

The sandals which will make a female of me belong to many women. The front of the temple entrance hides itself behind shoe-racks. Visitors enter barefooted, leaving behind the dung, dried frogs, spilled petrol and ketchup traces of the streets. Hundreds of pairs of gold and silver sandals wait here for the women who will re-emerge from the vigil with the taste of basil leaf and sugar in their deep-breathing mouths and carpet fibres between their toes. The sandals, gold and silver, seem all alike. How can the women tell them apart? They do tell them apart. It is as if each pair sings an intimate mantra to its owner, audible only to her. One day I too shall return to expectant slippers that stack up like the moon and the stars outside a marble building; one day I shall not have to wear child's shoes.

SUNDAY BEFORE SCHOOL: WHITE SNEAKERS

Seven years of these shoes are a chemical memory. The Convent ruled that pupils' shoes must be white: absolutely white. Who can imagine a 1980s shoe that was absolutely white, without any logo, with no swoosh, not a single slogan? Sunday evenings, before the school week,

I crouched down on the pink bathroom tiles and painted my shoes into the absolute of whiteness; like the Alice in Wonderland gardeners repainting roses. This task was performed with a toothbrush and with special paste that annihilated so many design features. Purity was attained by the application of a whitener that stank of scientific polysyllables. Convent-girl identity. Tabula rasa. Toxicity and intoxication: with good intentions, getting high on paste.

BAD MARRIAGE SHOES: SILVER BALLET SLIPPERS

When I met my ex, I was already committed to heels: black ankle boots with four-inch stacks for walking through snow; French cream curved suede stilettos for scaling fire-escape ladders on to rooftops to admire the winter sky; even after I left him, scarlet satin bedroom-only spiky mules to amuse myself. Early on, my ex said that the way women walk in heels looks ugly. And my nails made unnatural social appearances: emerald lacquer; cobalt; incarnadine. Sign of a bad marriage: I began to wear flats. The penitential mermaid shoes, worn once and once only, were a Gabor creation: distressed silver ballet slippers with netted and criss-cross side details which would make the material seem to swish with the changes of light on feet that go walking. Cool as moonlight on a tourist coastline. But the inner stitching hooked the softness of my skin which has always been too soft; but I could not turn back, for we had tickets to an evening of Mozart; but the paper tissues that I stuffed into my shoes failed to act as a protective lining. Paper tissue snowflecks teardropped with crimson blood created a trail behind me as I ascended the many tiers of the wedding-cake concert hall.

BAREFOOT: PEARL PINK POLISH

Sitting next to someone can make my feet curl: shy, self-destructive and oyster-like, they want to shuck their cases, to present themselves, little undersea pinks; their skin still is too soft, their toes still too long, their ankles still too slender, for a modern fit. But he is not modern; he sits like stone, and my bare feet are cool, they will not have to bleed.

4

Stalker

for KM Grant

He waits. Without knowing me,
he waits. The tips of branches,
edible and winey, bring
spring by suggestion to him
who in autumn dawn, eager,
with wet knees, disregards me,
being drawn by me. He waits
and in me he waits. I branch,
the form is branching, it bounds
like sight from dark to bright, back
again. The form is from me:
it is him, poem, stag, first sight
and most known. In him I wait:
(when he falls) needs must (hot heap),
nothing left over (treelike
no longer) nor forlorn: we're
totalled.

Ian Duhig

Blockbusters

> *'He lives in Leeds, completely out of the literary world.'*
> John Freeman, ex-Editor *Granta*

> *'Thrillers like* The Da Vinci Code *are key indicators*
> *of contemporary ideological shifts.'*
> Slavoj Žižek, *In Defence of Lost Causes*

For what might break the grip that held my pen
so fast I couldn't write another line
I quested through the shops of Lady Charity
in Urbs Leodiensis Mystica,
the Shed Crew's capital of Ashtrayland,
a town beyond the literary world
whose locals speak blank verse (says Harrison);
Back-to-Front Inside-Out Upside-Down Leeds,
according to the Nuttgens book I bagged –
along with others offering keys to open
secrets of iambic pentameter,
to them, a ball and chain, a waltz – or best,
in Žižek's windsock for the New World Order,
Gnostic code imprinted by five feet
that lead us to a grail Brown liquefies,
as Shakespeare sometimes turns this line himself
to deliquescent decasyllabics
like the blood of St Januarius.
Brown quotes from Philip's Gospel (where it suits)
to build on Rosslyn Chapel's premises
his castle perilously in the air
while staying blind to mysteries below,
such as why you'll see Rosslyn's masons carved
among the seven virtues Greed,
and then set Charity with deadly sins…
The world was made in error Philip wrote –

Savonarola, in *The Rule of Four*,
another blockbuster from Oxfam's shelves
that followed in the footprints of Dan Brown,
is made to quote 'the Gospel of St Paul'…
is this the fault of slipshod editing
or does it hint perhaps at secret truth?
What if 'Paul's Gospel' really did exist?
What if it was some long-lost Gnostic text
thrown on the Bonfire of the Vanities
but glimpsed once by our zealot's burning eyes
who then confided to the ancestors
of those that seemed just greedy novelists
a hidden road map to the Holy Grail
a blind man saw on his Damascus road?

My back-to-back looks on a blind man's road
that runs due north from here past Wilfrid's city,
Shandy Hall then on to Lindisfarne
whose monks St Wilfrid was once sent from Rome
to knock back into shape from toe to top,
their sinful tops being 'Simon Magus tonsures',
that Gnostic wizard and heresiarch
the dog denounces in St Peter's Acts,
where that saint brings smoked tuna back to life,
explains his crucifixion upside-down
and how God's Kingdom could be found on Earth:
Make right your left, back forwards, low your high,
a realm inverted on our retinas,
much like Creation in the Gnostic view –
then, in a flash, like Paul, I saw the light
through Peter's apophatic paradox
to Stevens' definition of a poem,
a mirror-image of Frost's melting ice,
the fiery self-consuming meteor
but one surviving as 'the stone from heaven',
Wolfram Von Eschenbach's holy grail –
and knowing this, my pen was free again

like that sword Arthur freed from its own block,
but mightier and greedy for the words
so close to silence they're worth more than gold.
My quest was ended: I began to write
this poem backwards, as Da Vinci might.

Bridled Vows

I will be faithful to you, I do vow,
but not until the seas have all run dry
et cetera. Although I mean it now
I'm not a prophet and I will not lie.

To be your perfect wife, I could not swear;
I'll love, yes; honour (maybe); won't obey,
but will co-operate if you will care
as much as you are seeming to today.

I'll do my best to be your better half,
but I don't have the patience of a saint
and at you, not with you, I'll sometimes laugh,
and snap too, though I'll try to show restraint.

We might work out. No blame if we do not.
With all my heart, I think it's worth a shot.

Choman Hardi

Dispute Over a Mass Grave

The one you have finished examining
is my son. That is the milky coloured Kurdish
suit his father tailored for him, the blue shirt
his uncle gave to him. Your findings prove
that it is him – he was a tall fifteen year old,
was left handed, had broken a rib.

I know she too has been looking for her son
but you have to tell her that this is not him.
Yes the two of them were playmates and fought
the year before. But it was my son who broke
a rib, hers only feigned to escape trouble.

That one is mine! Please give him back to me.
I will bury him on the verge of my garden –
the mulberry tree will offer him its shadow,
the flowers will earnestly guard his grave,
the hens will peck on his gravestone,
the beehive will hum above his head.

Researcher's Blues

Every day I try to lose them in the streets,
leave them behind in a bend in the road and keep on
walking. But they follow me everywhere, their voices
combining into a hum from which sentences rise and fall.
The woman I never interviewed cut the string of my sleep
at dawn, whispering: 'I am not well.' Why didn't I listen
to her story? Why didn't I realise that she was dying?
The one widowed at 26 told me, 'Imagine twenty
years of loneliness.' I remember her in the middle of
an embrace and start weeping. The pleading voice
of the woman who was raped echoes in my head:
'I only wanted bread for my son.' I wish I had told her
that she is good, she is pure, not spoiled as she thinks she is.
Then I remember the old couple in their mud-brick house,
surrounded by goats and chickens. I remember their tears
when they talk about their children, when they remember
a woman who had been rich and powerful in her own village
but in Nugra Salman 'she was stinking, abandoned,
worm-stricken'. What was the dead woman's name?
Why didn't I try to find her family? I keep walking away.
All I want is to walk without crying, without being
pitied by people who think that I have problems
with love, without the homeless man telling me that he is
sorry. I want to disappear, be unnoticed, unpitied.
Sometime ago when I started, it was all clear. I knew
what had to be done. All I can do now is keep walking,
carrying this sorrow in my soul, all I can do is
pour with grief which has no beginning and no end.

Alice Oswald

Flies

This is the day the flies fall awake mid-sentence
and lie stunned on the window-sill shaking with speeches
only it isn't speech it is trembling sections of puzzlement which
break off suddenly as if the questioner had been shot

this is one of those wordy days
when they drop from their winter quarters in the curtains
    and sizzle as they fall
feeling like old cigarette butts called back to life
blown from the surface of some charred world

and somehow their wings which are little more than flakes
    of dead skin
have carried them to this blackened disembodied question

what dirt shall we visit today?
what dirt shall we re-visit?

they lift their faces to the past and walk about a bit
trying out their broken thought-machines
coming back with their used-up words

there is such a horrible trapped buzzing wherever we fly
it's going to be impossible to think clearly now until next winter
what should we
what dirt should we

Slowed-Down Blackbird

Three people in the snow
getting rid of themselves
      breath by breath

and every six seconds a blackbird

three people in raincoats losing their tracks in the snow
walking as far as the edge and back again
with the trees exhausted
      tapping at the sky

and every six seconds a blackbird

first three then two
passing one eye between them
and the eye is a white eraser rubbing them away

and on the edge a blackbird
trying over and over its broken line
trying over and over its broken line

Denise Riley

Listening for lost people

Still looking for lost people – look unrelentingly.
'They died' is not an utterance in the syntax of life
where they belonged, no *belong* – reanimate them
not minding if the still living turn away, casually.
Winds ruck up its skin so the sea tilts from red-blue
to blue-red: into the puckering water go his ashes
who was steadier than these elements. Thickness
of some surviving thing that sits there, bland. Its
owner's gone nor does the idiot howl – while I'm
unquiet as a talkative ear. Spring heat, a cherry
tree's fresh bronze leaves fan out and gleam – to
converse with shades, yourself become a shadow.
The souls of the dead are the spirit of language:
you hear them alight inside that spoken thought.

The patient who had no insides

i The ins and outs of it

As clouds swell to damply fill gaps in mountains, so in
Illness we sense, solidly, our entrails expanding to stuff
That space of our innerness just feebly imagined before.

I'd slumped at home before the nightly documentaries
Of scalpels nipping through the primrose fat, beaded
With that orange hue that blood becomes on camera,

But only when they crossly assert themselves do those
Guts I hadn't believed in, truly come home in me.
Figuratively, yes, we've guts – literally, may suspect

We haven't – poking sceptical as Doubting Thomases
For what's packed below skin we don't see laid bare.
Invaginated folds, ballooning orifices, we know about

And pregnancy, watching some unborn other's heels
Nudging and butting like carp snouts under the navel.
That's someone else altogether, palpable inside me.

No, it's my disbelief in my own entrails that I mean.
I'd glimpsed the radiographer's dark film, starring
Barium-whitened swags of colon, mine. Blown glass,

Hooped entrails ridged with their glazed diverticules
Like little suckers studded plumply on squid tentacles
Of my intestines. But now I see their outer evidence:

My ginger skin. How well you look, they'd said to me
At work. But no tan browned my face. The malady
Conveyed an air of robust health through bronzing me.

Now foamy bracken-brown urine cools in plastic jugs
For measuring on the ward, frothed like a hillside stream
Relaxing into pools. 'What says the doctor to my water?'

Jaundice is read as if the humours still remained reliable.
There were insides inside me – now they've gone all wrong.
Modern regimes of signs set in, and newly prudent thoughts

That what they stamp, we own. Pointers to a depth, to be
'Philosophically, Medicinally, Historically open'd & cut up'.
From Burton's ripe account of melancholy, that last quote.

The sorrows brood inside our purplish spleens, barriers
That check dark moods of sultry bile by segregating it
Where it can't seep to hurt us. Anatomised emotion.

'Pancreas' means 'all flesh'. Now, awry, it chews itself.
That piece of ambient meat I am eats meaty me all up.
Enzymes flood to champ their host, their prey – that's

Me. They don't know where to stop. I'm auto-gesting.
Spontaneous combustion in a schlock Victorian engraving
Of hearthrug scorched, charred ankles jutting out of boots,

No more of faithful Lizzie left. A hapless autophage I am
Whose fizzog has gone bad. Enzymes digesting tissue grind
In rampant amylase and swollen lipase counts. Sure signs

Affecting the liver, a plush nursery for the vegetal spirit.
Fondly this warming organ clasps the stomach set over it
Fingering heat into it, nursing its charge, so Galen held.

Flame-like, this liver, slow-cooking the stomach's stuff
Down to a bloodlike juice. Not boiling it dry to char it
Or simmering it to gruel – if the liver's temper is right.

Noble the strong liver, 'dark monarch' to Neruda.
But ignoble, the long slim pear of the gall bladder
And the sole-like spleen, roughened, its shoe shape

Splayed into an ox tongue. Spleen, milky-pulped
Innocent home to the darkest of humours, frees all
Merriment in its bearer, by holding black bile apart

And so, wrote Harvey, 'the spleen causes one to laugh'.
Dreaming of red things, the sanguine man keeps bluff,
Night dreads held safely at bay. Splenetic laughter!

'Remembering mine affliction and my misery
The wormwood and the gall.' So cries Lamentations
Too harsh on the house of that yellow emulsifier,

Hard too on wormwood – a friend, boiled to absinthe,
To smoky Verlaine, and the maker of Pernod's fortune.
Antique are that shrubby vermifuge's properties: bitter

Carminative, anthelmintic, cholagogue, febrifuge,
Swelling the secretion of both liver and gall bladder.
Bluish or red-brown skin markings today? Bad signs.

iii The patient longs to know

Back on the ward, the darting housemen, veering,
Swerve low by ends of beds like swifts, but then zoom off.
Come back! the impatient patient wails, though silently,

Why am I 'nil by mouth' for endless days? Am I each day
Prepped for some other op which never comes – or what?
Unreadable as a leaving lover, no houseman stops to say.

'Your notes got lost so we might send you back, pre-op.
Without your write-up, no, the anaesthetist won't like it.'
My starved heart sinks at hearing this; it's bodily starved

Like all the rest of me, so long on 'nil by mouth'. Nil
In my own mouth, yes, to eat or drink – but also nil
Issued as word of explanation from a doctor's mouth.

Let me go home so I can find things out. Googling
Fulfils the nineteenth century's dream of ardent enquiry
Amassed, and nearly democratically. On medics' sites

The grand Miltonic phrases of the biliary tract race home:
Islets of Langerhans, Ampulla of Yater, Duct of Santorini,
Sphincter of Oddi. Sonorous names, some the narrowings

Which, blocked, can cause grave trouble. They had for me;
That gall bladder, choked, must go. But will its ghost
Kick up in me, once it is tossed away? This oddness of

Owning spare parts. Our bodies littered with redundancies,
Walking reliquaries rattling our appendices, blunt tails,
Primordial. For we are birds with teeth and empty crops.

iv *The consultant summarises our national health*

'Liver, until so recently the Cinderella of medicine!
Just the girl in the clinical ashes, unrescued as yet,
Assailed by her bad suitors – weak policies and folly.

'Alcohol-led liver failure rising, bile duct cancer rates
Mounting, more cirrhosis from viral illness, Hep B, C.
More drinking, younger drinking, increased steatosis,

'Yet funders don't cough up for self-induced sickness.
Specialists get scarcer, beds vanish, bureaucracy swells
As need begs for new transplants, more artificial livers.

'One gets despondent. Lifestyle's the problem,' adds
This eminent hepatologist, despondent at 'patching up
Self-harming patients, worsened by government policy'.

His time is short. This patient nods and leaves. So
It's our national fantasy, not just my private idiocy,
That what our daily intake is by mouth has nil effect?

v Discharged

'Your liver tests are squiffy, Mrs R, but you might
As well go home, you won't get well in here' – then
He's darted off again, mercurial houseman. Outside
The well ones all charge past us like young bullocks,
Amazingly confident. Those who were ill go gingerly.
A smack of post-ward colour shoves us back to life.

Shortlisted Poems
The Felix Dennis Prize for
Best First Collection

Nancy Campbell

Malinguartoq / The dance

The hunter is a drunken fool;
    he bets, but rarely pays.
To win, he will break every rule
    in every game he plays.

The hunter wears a coat of skin
    and picks his blistered nose.
He won't remove his thrice-lined boots
    or change his underclothes.

He fumbles with a fraying cord
    to keep his temper calm.
The ends are knotted together,
    encircling his palm,
and his torn black nails weave in and out
    tangling the oily yarn.

Sometimes he sits so silently
    I forget that he is there
and I laugh and sing and sigh for him
    and unbraid my long black hair.

They say he was born too early,
    a caul upon his head.
I know his blood and mine run close,
    too close by far to wed,
yet I have lain all night with him
    in the narrow iron bed.

The animals watch for the hunter,
    but last night I saw him throw
the gloves of skin I sewed for him
    down to the dogs in the snow.

The old wounds open and start to weep
    on the hunter's hairless hands.
I ask why blood continues to seep
    though I staunch it with a band,
but he only mutters in his sleep
    those words I don't understand.

He travels miles across the ice
    yet never leaves his bed.
His cheeks are growing hollow;
    his eyes stare far ahead.

The animals wait. They are hungry
    but they trust he will follow the rest,
with an amulet in place of a gun
    clutched to his cold, clean chest.

The hunter's wife becomes the sun

'Don't go without this.' Isabel handed me a small white box
which held a candlestick and four attendant angels.
Jingling clichés punched from sheets of tin,
the angels turn, propelled by heat rising from a candle,
and hooked by their haloes from wires as if the darkness
were a deep pool for fly-fishing, and my window

delicate as ice upon its surface. Spinning by the window,
this carousel recalls a childhood blessing: *Four angels
at my head.* If they came to life, like the small white angels
who fought the Snow Queen's snowflakes, would their tin
armour frighten bears back to the polar darkness?
Whose are the gifts they grasp: tree, star, trumpet, candle?

Only the undertaker sells the right kind of candle
to suit these angels. At home, he wreathes a small white coffin
with plastic lilies, but says nothing. His window
overlooks crucifixes buried in snow; there are no angels
on the graves of the Danes, who came to barter tin
for ivory and sealskin. Their eyes brimmed with darkness,

you see it in old photographs. Sleepless in the darkness,
I read their letters home, those 'tragic accidents'. Green candles
burn beyond the hills: the dead are dancing. The window
between the worlds grows thin. A solar wind blows its low tin whistle
and fire draws closer. Soon Earth will be a small white dwarf,
a revolving toy abandoned by its guardian angels.

The candle gutters. Lynched in their own light, the angels
hang still. Each holds her gift before her as if the tin
scorched her fingertips. Heat has melted the small white stump
to nothing. Once, they say, this land was lit by candles
made of ice, when water burned, glazing the darkness
of endless night. Day had not dawned on any window.

The hunter spoke. His cold breath quenched a candle:
'In darkness we are without death.' His wife listened
and replied, 'But we need more light, not darkness,
while we are alive.' She seized a shard of incandescent ice
and rose into the sky, scattering a vast white wake
of stars, which some might say were angels,

if, in temperate darkness, we still believed in angels.
The small seal and the white whale know we're just tin gods.
At the world's last window, I light another candle.

Ron Carey

Upstairs

Lying on the bed with my mother,
Wearing my father's Alpaca overcoat.
Here, Upstairs, where the air is old
And the blue-painted radiators are singing
And the cold cream is liquefying on the dressing table.
My mother can no longer take the cold.

My father was my age when he died.
I look like him everyone says I look SO like him everyone says.
I had to think when she asked me to wear the coat,
For a moment I had to think about it like I didn't know what she
   meant.
It was then she called me Danny too many times Danny she called me.
Please, Danny, she said.
So I put on the coat.

She wants to lie down the pain for a moment, just for a moment,
On to the pink candlewick spread, Upstairs, where her body will not
   take her.
So I lift her in my arms. So light. Oh! Sarah you are SO light. I
   carry her.
Up. To the age before one is old.
Up where Sarah and Danny once moved in the fluid
Of young bodies and slept, hot to the touch.

We pretend to sleep, Danny and me,
Though I sweat in the coat and I don't feel well.
But I stay still, for Sarah's sake I am still.
The afternoon seagulls are mad at something in the garden.
I should investigate because they sound so near and real and mad
   but I can't
Because she will not let go of his hand.

After a while, released into the darkness, I get up.
I see very little by the nibbling light of the Sacred Heart.
Sarah. Softly.
Sarah. Quietly.
Sarah. My father's voice.
And she says nothing she says, nothing.
Leaving me, afraid
That everything might be said and done and said
And she has taken all the cold of the earth into herself.

The Murderer's Dog

It came towards us as if the world was still
The same; tail-thumping the summer grass.
A boy next to me shouted, *It's His dog!*
A hail of stones followed it down the road.

We chased it into fields of gorse and bracken
Where, squeezing through gaps half the size
Of its body, it hung pieces of its sleek coat.
Late in the evening it turned towards Town.

It ran up Main Street; breaking the quiet fix
Of the Church, past the Police Station, past
Other dogs, barking mad in their flower-filled
Prisons; past the house of the dead child.

John Joe's mother scrambled onto the road.
Here! Help me! It's here. Here! Quick!
We stampeded through the house, shaking
China cups from dreams of immortality.

In the long shadows of Gleeson's backyard
It stood at bay, its legs in a barbed confusion
Of wire. When it saw us it howled in despair.
After a while it stopped and lay in the dirt.

Compassion moved among us, searching
Each nameless heart. But then it rolled its lips
Into a hideous, wolfish smile, revealing at last
Its true nature – the nature of its master.

Someone should have warned it not to snarl
Or snap; that it only made things worse.
Andy handed me a shovel thick with mud.
I brought it down hard, with all my strength.

Before we left it at the door of the dead child,
We dragged it through the streets on the steel
Palm of the shovel; showers of sparks falling
Like meteorites in the dark planet of its eye.

Harry Giles

Brave

Acause incomer will aywis be a clarty wird,
acause this tongue A gabber wi will nivver be the real
  Mackay, A sing.
Acause fer aw that we're aw Jock Tamson's etcetera, are we
  tho? Eh? Are we.
Acause o muntains, castles, tenements n backlans,
acause o whisky exports, acause o airports,
acause o islans, A sing.
acause o pubs whit arena daein sae weel oot o the smokin
  ban, A sing.
acause hit's grand tae sit wi a lexicon n a deeskit mynd, A
  sing.
acause o the pish in the stair, A sing.
acause o ye,

A sing o a Scotland whit wadna ken workin class
  authenticity gin hit cam reelin aff an ile rig douned six
  pints o Tennent's n glasst hit in the cunt,
        whit hit wadna
                by the way.

A sing o google Scotland,
        o laptop Scotland,
                o a Scotland sae dowf on bit-torrentit HBO
                drama series n DLC packs fer
                paistapocalyptic RPGs that hit wadna ken
                hits gowk fae hits gadjie,
                        tae whas lips n fingers amazebawz cams
                        mair freely as bangin.

A sing o a Scotland whit hinks the preservation o an
  evendoun Scots leeteratur is o parteecular vailyie n
  importance bit cadna write hit wi a reproduction claymore
  shairp on hits craig,
              whit hinks Walter Scott scrievit in an either tide,
              whit hinks Irvine Welsh scrievit in an either tide.

A sing o a Scotland whit wants independence fae Tories
              n patronisin keeks
                      n chips on shoulders
                              bit sprattles tae assert ony kin o
                              cultural autonomy whit isna
                              grundit in honeytraps.

A sing o a Scotland whit hinks thare's likely some sort o
  God, richt?
              whit wad like tae gang fer sushi wan nicht but cadna
              haundle chopsticks,
              whit signs up fur internet datin profiles n nivver
              replies tae the messages,
              whit dreams o bidin in London.

A sing o a Scotland whit fires tourists weirin See You Jimmy
  hats the puir deathstare,
              n made a pynt o learnin aw the varses tae Auld
              Lang Syne,
                      n awns a hail signed collection o Belle n
                      Sebastian EPs.

A sing o a Scotland bidin in real dreid o wan day findin oot
  juist hou parochial aw hits cultural references mey be,
              n cin only cope wi the intertextuality o the Scots
              Renaissance wi whappin annotatit editions,
                      n weens hits the same wi awbdy else.

A sing o a Scotland whit hasna gied tae Skye,
      or Scrabster,
            or Scone,
                        bit cin do ye an absolute dymont o
                        a rant on the plurality o Scots
                        identity fae Alexandair mac
                        Alexandair tae Wee Eck.

A sing o a Scotland whit cadna hink o a grander wey tae
   end a nicht as wi a poke o chips n curry sauce,
         whit chacks the date o Bannockburn on
         Wikipaedia,
         whit's no sae shuir aboot proportional
         representation,
         whit draws chairts on the backs o beermats tae
         learn ye aboot rifts n glaciation
                  n when hit dis hit feels this oorie dunk,
                              this undesairvt wairmth
                                    o inexplicable luve,
         whit is heavt up,
                  in the blenks afore anxiety is heavt up
                        by the lithe curve o a firth.
         Whit wants ye tae catch the drift.
         Whit's stairtin tae loss the pynt.

A sing o a Scotland whit'll chant hits hairt oot dounstairs
   o the Royal Oak, whit'll pouk hits timmer clarsach
   hairtstrangs, whit like glamour will sing hits hairt intae
   existence, whit haps sang roon hits bluidy nieve hairt,

         whit sings.

The Hairdest Man in Govanhill

The hairdest man in Govanhill has thay lang white scairs on
  baith sides o his mooth fae smilin that damn wide.
>   He tint twa teeth fae brushin ower sterly
>   n his lips are gelt fae kissin babbies.
>   His vyce shifts bus routes.

The hairdest man in Govanhill has airms like rebar fae
  cartin aboot auld folks' messages.
>   He spits that haird hit colfs potholes.
>   He pisses that haird hit dichts stairwalls
>   blast-cleans
>   n hit smells o roses n aw.
>   He fairts that haird hit blaws the cloods fae the lift
>   n the sun skyres haird on Victoria Street.

The hairdest man in Govanhill had tae stap playin fitba
  acause whanivver he fungt the baw hit brust
>   but he'll staund in fer a missin goal post
>   ithoot ye e'en askin.

The hairdest man in Govanhill can gar Cooncillors tae tell
  the truith
>   juist by turnin his een in thair airtin
>   fae up tae eleiven miles awa.

The hairdest man in Govanhill is that haird that whiles
  whan he reads the news
>   sittin in his airmchair in the mids o the junction
>   he juist
>   greets
>   pal, juist
>   greets

n the puils o his tears stap traffic
n weans sweem in thaim
n he greets hairder juist tae please thaim
        or mebbe at the sheer existence o thair
        lauchter in this warld
            oi
                aye
                        this warld.

His chin is that haird he skives wi a risp n has a contract wi
    Brillo fer the clippins.
His feet are that haird Sustrans fee him tae fletten oot bike
    paiths wharivver thay fancy.
His nose is that haird hit cheesels the names o the deid on a
    hunner-year-auld heidstane.
His hair is that haird he gies hit tae canal-boats fer sweeng
    raips.
He's that bluidy haird he's a hairt tattooed wi Dulux on his
    bicep n aw hit says is *A LUV YE.*

When the hairdest man in Govanhill staps up tae ye n
    luiks ye haird in the ee n says in dymont soonds – *A'm the
hairdest man in Govanhill* – he means
        Aye.
                Youse n aw.

Ruby Robinson

Undress

There is an ash tree behind this house. You
can see it from our bedroom window.
If you stare at it for long enough, you'll see
it drop a leaf. Stare at it now, you said,
and notice the moment a leaf strips away
from its branch, giving a twirl. Consider this.

The ash tree unclothes itself Octoberly.
From beside our bed, fingering the curtain,
observe the dark candles at the top of
that tree, naked and alert, tending to the breeze.
A sheet of ice between the rooftops
and this noiseless sky has turned the air

inside out. Black veins of branches
shake against the blue screen on which they
hang. Small mammals are hibernating
in pellets of warm air under ground. But,
in spite of the cold, this ash tree does not shy
from shrugging off its coat, sloping its nude

shoulders to the night. So, you said, undo,
unbutton, unclasp, slowly remove. Let down your
hair, breathe out. Stand stark in this room until
we remember how not to feel the chill.
Stand at the window, lift your arms right up
like a tree. Yes – like that. Watch leaves drop.

Apology

I can't go up because I don't know how.
Nobody has shown me.

So many names, my mother, I'm never sure
  what to call you. So many names for all your predators
  and crushes and suitors. I'm sorry.

I'm sorry I'm here and I'm sorry I'm not here.
  Would you have made it on your own
  without the comorbid condition of motherhood
  and the slowness and consistency of time?

I'm sorry for the slowness and consistency of time;
  years like zombies dawdling toward a cliff edge
  holding back the child's writhing body, itching to grow, packed
  around the same mind I have now.

I'm sorry the concept of promise outgrew the concept of child
  and that systemic contradiction and wizardry left only a dim
  sense of suspicion; a crescending breeze, accumulating clouds
  amidst bewildering dichotomies.

I'm sorry for resembling your relatives and captors and the man
  who penetrated you, who's still there, communicating boldly
  via intersections of others' thought waves and memories,
  blatant into the long nights, haunting,

  for my inferiority in the face of nuclear family culture,
  feeding on detritus of white goods, leisure sports, laminate floors,
  a real home and fake recycling,

  for creeping by night into a tight void, blinds down, brain blown
  glass-thin, electric impulses and bloated thoughts bolted in.
  For this life being the only one my quiet mind knows,

its many versions and phases, I'm sorry. I wasn't your daughter
– or anyone – when you were the blue-water navy,
or the beheaded, or the baby boy. Or was I?

I'm sorry I was not yet born and could not yet hear you
when you were over there, listening carefully
for the rain and small movements of animals, for sounds
of life, through a green, five-fingered haze.

I'm sorry I consider sentiment, fact; authenticity, originality,
when they are irrelevant. So many choices
in supermarkets, the natural habitat of panic attacks,
it's enough to make anyone sorry and I am.

I'm sorry it's taking over half a century to link your purple-patched
brain scan to the basic biology of stress. The piano thunders on,
sustain pedal wired to the facial muscles of all your neglecters,
aching like hell behind their stamina and machinery.

I'm sorry I had, logically, to think of my own self first / simultaneously,
navigating through the fire and acid of Trust and her sycophant
Love before returning. All the powerful were women; the power
of penises and facial hair originated there, cajoled by matriarchs.

As if skin and breath were insignificant! I'm so sorry.
Where are you now, to take into my arms and resuscitate?
Is it too late, given you're fifty and no longer a child?

It's always mothers and mind control which is why
I thank you for breaking the cycle, withstanding the enormity
of generations, magnetic as water, to let us go. You weren't to know

about other outrageous families and sadistic counterparts.
A nugget of my limbic system remembered choosing my own
lemon-yellow baby clothes so thank you.

I squeezed that into the thumb-sized space
in the palm of my hand knowing all along they were wrong
and imploding with it.

I'm sorry I wept in the shower for your cancelled wedding,
  letting the violet dress down the plughole, unsure
  what it all meant except things staying the same, *future*
  aggravating my brain, a baby brother gone again.

I'm sorry you were out there, alone, defined by the worst
  of others and defined by your children's prisms of hope
  and survival mechanisms. In one version, you did marry and lived
  in a house with green walls and extravagant furniture.

I'm sorry that consensus reality had you set fire to your bed
  as you lay in it; arrested, put in a cell, let off the next day
  because the lawyer believed it was a genuine attempt
  and convinced the police.

I'm sorry you've had to withstand such torrents
  of knowledgeless advice and legal toxification,
  clinging to reality by a sinew of tooth, remembering yourself,
  through the rough and the smooth.

I'm sorry I was absent, memorising books of the Bible
  for a bar of Dairy Milk, owning up to things
  I'd never done, getting confirmed as an antidote
  to the evil core of me.

I'm sorry it was exotic to think of kids like me
  ending up in prison, coincidentally, inevitably
  or prevented (which is the same), salvaged, peristalsised
  through society, brain safely contained,

  doused daily in cold water or electricity
  or disgrace, temptations kept consistently far enough away
  as to appear illusory

like you, my brave mother, fantastic prodigy
in flowing white kaftan, knotted long brown hair, a beautiful gaze
of solemnity, rare stone, emotionless (defined by others).

I'm sorry I was ill-prepared for your soiled mattress
and comatose body, under a wave of advocaat
and transistor radios oozing with cheap Scotch. Even I
developed feelings for them amidst adults acting like it's okay

to leave you this way, the bluebottles in on it,
inflated with dog shit and red hot egos, resting on your cheek,
your lip, too cunning to get rid of.

I'm sorry that laughing off a difficult childhood
didn't make it never happen. Even a basic calculator
recognises an infinite loop as a malfunction; don't they see *cutting
off my privates every night* needs additional information?

I'm sorry I talked you out of wounding yourself
although I know it feels hopeful and lets in sunlight and air
through an open door. I'm sorry I can't help you go up.
I, also, don't know how.

I'm sorry I prioritise the stimulation of adrenalin and opioids
in my own axis before I come to you. Thank you
for believing I love you even though you know
I don't know love or trust it.

I dreamed a baby died from kidney failure. The worst part?
Not knowing distress from relief in the face of the mother,
like a child in an experiment. What does this mean?

My man fearing a moment of madness. Not locking the
knives away but keeping a steady eye on them, paying attention
to the moon and turning moods. He underestimates me;

I'm my own doppelgänger. Here I am, locked to him, discussing
sex positions and holiday destinations. Here I am
courting solitude in the doorway, a pair of eyes and a chest cavity

thrumming on the dark boundary between survival and self-control.
While there are no babies, I carry on. I am testament to the
    problem
of the baby. Look at me – flaunting my own survival. Who am I?

Except the parasite that accidentally caught on
to your womb wall as you lay stoned on a fur-lined coat
in a hallway in Moss Side? *Happy accident, accidentally on purpose.*

Close the piano lid. Empty a drawer. Things happen.

I'm sorry for absences, holidaying in France, studying guilt,
    time-travelling the pain barrier, intent on nerve endings
    and their connections to various biological systems.
    Learning to accept and relinquish responsibility appropriately.

Throwing back the hot stone in a horizontal line.

Thank you to the policeman who took all the men whose safety
    you feared for to the pub so you could come home
    for dinner, monologue, nail-varnish remover, a set
    of impartial weighing scales and cheap French wine.

I'm sorry about the home, the wine, the monologue resonating
    against the plastic mug others might keep for you, fussing
    over make-up-smeared walls, upholstery and understatements.
    I'm a bit sad we can't see Al. He comes on the radio sometimes.

I'm sorry I'm not bringing you home, finally, to thrive and repair.
    I wanted to stay, singing Luther Vandross on the walkway
    outside at 6 a.m., fetching toast from the neighbour. I was hoping
    for perfection, *believing in anything*, all those years.

Is it too ambitious to hope? I'm sentimentally sorry
despite a genuine fear of sentimentality and pseudo-unhappiness,
struggling under the weight of an A1 poster on complex trauma

and a pair of Sennheiser headphones to lock me in.
*Think of what it is when God himself puts his arms around you
and says "welcome home."* There's nothing mysterious

about my thoughts or affect, nor yours, nor anyone's, biologically
generated by the relationships we hide our consciousness from.
Oh unhappiness and infidelity! Disguised in metaphor

you're nothing but the deep yearning of an infant for its mother
and the furiousness. Making this connection is like remembering
being born, which is like folding time, which is no one to blame and
all the world to blame.

Thank you for picking up the handless, footless doll
in the park, saving him from a dog or fox or thoughtless children,
keeping him to your breast on the tram, the bus, in pubs
and not noticing the scathing looks.

I learnt to trust without you, leaving my thoughts
outside for five minutes and trusting the neighbour's cat
not to urinate on them.

I'm sorry my stand-in mother was an evil replica, machine-like
yet unpredictable. We tried to calculate an algorithm for her
mood, as you would've done, and in 14 years never cracked it.
She remained seated when I left for the last time.

You weren't to know
and they wouldn't have believed you anyway.
We learn to accept the clouds for what they are
and wait, patiently.

Tiphanie Yanique

Zuihitsu for the day I cheat on my husband, to my fiancé

I will write
in my journal:

"My lover is warm to my body. Like hair, he covers me.

I could remember my husband meeting me on the mountain. Hitching with another man's wife. This is before he is my husband. On the phone, I tell him: when you arrive, please grab me and hold me. And then when he and the wife arrive I see her first. She is beautiful and my heat is eager. When I see my husband, who is not yet my husband, he opens his arms like oars. Cleaves me onto him and lowers me. Everyone is watching!

I will say my husband is like skin. The imperfect container of things. Yes, shedding, but always growing back.

Skin: When it splits, there is bleeding. When it breaks, the vitals tumble out.

Will I call him Baby?

I could remember the time my cousin, in her effort to inherit the house, locked our old aunt out so she would die. I could recall how my husband, who is not yet my husband, held my head in his lap as I howled against the fireworks – their beauty bursting – though nothing but light and gunshots, into the horror of what family can be.

The lover will be the kind that blows his horn and makes my body shake and sing. "Oh Baby!" I will call out when I'm coming.

Perhaps wives who have sex with men not their husbands are afraid of growing old. Not to themselves, but to someone else. This is what I believe. It is nice to be a princess to someone again after being the queen.

Queen: The title a husband gives to his wife only after first giving it to his own mother.

I could remember, at a time I was deciding which man to marry, that I watched the film *Bridges of Madison County* with one of my possible husbands. I wept. Thinking, already, of the day this one would become the lover. Mourning already, the pummelled beauty of our affair. This one, who would not become my husband, asked why I cried so, and I could not tell him that I would not marry him but that I would take him as a lover when a lonely day came.

My husband, who is not yet my husband, says family is just people. Why expect anything else from them but what you can expect from people? And I say, but I want you to be my family. This is how I propose.

Husband: Next of kin.

Will the lover ever call me Baby?

The best love stories are the ones of infidelity. Faithfulness is a narrative so small. This is why, my husband will say, polyamory seems unpoetic. Jealousy loses its only use. The metaphor is more like having children, whom in vain you vow to love equally. Loving a spouse, says my husband who is not yet my husband, is like praising One God, whom you will betray. In the end, all the others are glittering lumps of fake gold. This is called sin.

Adultery: A fetish for monogamists.

I will tell Baby that I do not want people. I want family. Your husband, he will say, is your family, right? And I cannot tell if he is directing me to remain unattached or if he is pleading with me to adopt him.

My husband, who is not yet my husband, brought flowers. On the stairs, we kissed like the lost. Then he watched me walk into the subway and said, I can't wait to fuck you. It was our first date.

Perhaps, men who have sex with other men's wives are skimpy on soul. Their spines too fragile to carry folk on their own. They love prodigally. Still, I will fall for the lover and fuck him because that is what we wives do."

When I am found out I will say to my husband:

Marriage is a form of worship.

Altar Call

'If you bring forth what is within you,
what is within you will save you.'
　　　from *The Gnostic Gospel of St. Thomas*

The first time the man left her he walked down the aisle,
his face blank with hopelessnes or with hope.

The preacher had begged for those who wanted Jesus,
and so he was headed towards the altar.

The wife whispered, "Wait, my love,"
but that was not enough up against God calling him come.

That night the man asked her to pray with him.
He recited, as he alway did, the Our Father.

She performed the Hail Mary for him
and he lay in her lap like a child.

She claimed him as her bright little boy.
For after the altar, he could not be her man.

For years he believed he would grant her
a mansion, even though he never

managed half their tiny rent.
She learned that truth

was not what he could stand
and so he was never told that the landlord

was her lover. He was never told
that their son, slow, took after him.

The story of their life together
is the same as anyone's.

Shortlisted Poems
The Forward Prize for Best Single Poem

Sasha Dugdale

from **Joy**

The walls are wordless. There is a clock ticking.

I have woken up from a dream of abundant colour
and joy

I see his face and he is a shepherd and a piper and
a god

I see him bent by the grate, setting the fire, and he
is a fallen demon

I see him listening to the wind and sorrowing

I see wrath and misery, fire and desolation

A thousand fires in ancient London

And then the grass comes silent silent with the
hardest colour of all

The mirth colour the corn colour the summer
night colour

A thousand thousand summer nights pass

And children weave their daisy chains and place
them on the heads of fallen idols

He wept he wept more tears than there were days

And never chained the door lest, he said, we drive
an angel from it

And every morning he dipped his brush in wrath
and mildness

And out of him tumbled the biggest things of all

All of them righter than the rightest calculation

And truer than any compass

Yet where they were right and true none could say

And how they were right and true none could guess

But I knew I knew

He was an eye, and the eye wept and frowned and
smiled

The eye watched

The eye watered

The world was a mote in that eye

The mote was a world in that eye

And his brush was a blade and his tears made a
lake.

How I ache how I ache

Pause

Sole partner and sole part of all these joyes he read
to me in the summer house where we sat when Mr
Butts came knocking and found us naked reading
as we read every warm day the poor man liked to

tell that story to everyone as proof of the wildness
of our life though it never did seem wild to me but
consistent in all respects and full of holy sobriety
which looks to the untrained eye like wild joy

William stood then and made a deep bow to Satan
who had been watching and said you are welcome
to our garden sir

Satan had a round sad face like a waterwheel and
seemed tired and full of pity, he wore his rainbow
snake around him and when he saw we meant him
no harm he bowed and shrivelled to a vapour

But Mr Butts came in and ate some grapes

Pause

Have no fear Satan, said William, we will not harm
you

Yet all about us

War drifted from year to year like the seeds of
weeds in autumn

And the looms made sails for warships, and the
furnaces cast cannon balls

Men trained their horses to run towards death

all around us in schools and churches and meeting
halls

corpses marched their filthy regular steps

And men spoke about it and the words themselves
in pain, the words thirsty

For new life, the words wanted mercy

and in the midst of all this a clearing in Lambeth
and South Molton Street and Fountain Court and a
torrent of such wrathful innocence pours forth,
such light that violence staggered, violence fell
back

a spider a worm a beetle could approach it

but violence could not

an ant could find his children by it

but violence could not

And I tended that light

And he was the light

Rachel Hadas

Roosevelt Hospital Blues

I thought that nothing ever happened to me.
To other people, yes, but not to me.
But baby, I was as wrong as I could be.

I slipped on the ice last January, broke my wrist.
Thinking about you, slipped and broke my wrist.
Forgot how long it was since I'd been kissed.

February, March – we grabbed the hours we could.
My wrist was in a cast but we grabbed what time we could.
It was never enough but it was always good.

April in Haiti: we visited some schools.
Went to Haiti, visited three high schools.
Back in the hotel, swam in a turquoise pool.

A tree grew by the pool, its fruit was gold.
A nameless tree, its fruit was glowing gold.
Let's live together until we're really old.

My red bathing suit was drying on the bedspread.
We'd been making love all over the bed.
I want to live with you till we are dead.

They stoned this artist to death right in the street.
At thirty-one he died in a Petionville street.
Death is cold and life is full of heat.

The eyes he painted stare from the other side.
Those eyes: a challenge from the other side.
They say: I'm dead but my spirit hasn't died.

The lawyer in mascara looking like a raccoon,
The divorce lawyer disguised as a raccoon
Roots in a garbage pail under the moon.

Went to the doctor, didn't like what he said.
We held hands and listened to what the doctor said.
As long as I'm with you I'm not afraid.

He told me to go to Roosevelt Hospital ER,
Rush hour in the rain to the ER.
I hailed a rickshaw – next best thing to a car.

Riding in a rickshaw up Tenth Avenue,
Peddling in a rickshaw up Tenth Avenue,
My CAT scan sucks but I'm in love with you.

Love is a rickshaw bumping along in the rain,
Our love is a ride over potholes in the rain.
It's too intense, don't ask me to explain.

We're on some journey sweet and fast and slow,
Some adventure moving fast then slow.
Let's go together, baby, wherever we go.

David Harsent

from **Salt**

He cleared snow from the path and laid down salt.
He was conscious of oxygen, then: the word, also the way
his breath came back at him as mist to leave a trace
of ice on his upper lip. This shortly after dawn,
the sleepers in the house fixed like the dead, except the one
who turned in her dream looking for elbow-room, her voice
just short of reaching him, the snowfall soundless white, the salt
finding its way, the scuff of his boots in all that ghostliness.

A thickness in every breath.
The streets are white under hard sunlight.
'Where my shadow falls just short of me…'

Low skies bringing rain in off the sea, the deep odour
of wet tarmac. How often have you been here before:
those two on the boardwalk going in step, an old man
waiting to cross, the girl muffled in blue,
hand raised to flag a taxi… actors edging the real.

The agéd primagravida does the splits. Forceps are brought.
Her world of pain is such that she stands aside
to watch as the child is born to a season of rain and wind.
Selfhood is everything. Like mother, like son.

In that tiny diorama, she waits at the open door.
She is perfect: nails and lips and hair. The windows
carry reflections of hills, and a river that seems to flow.
She has never been to such a place.
How can there live such loneliness in her?

'Without salt flesh gathers worms; and though flesh be our foe
we are commanded to sustain it. And we must afflict it.
Habete, inquit, sal in vobis.' Offer me salt in every sacrifice.

'Seabirds': he spoke out loud to start the memory up.
Then 'Something in the sky', by which he meant
rain coming in from the unnaturally bright
seam of the horizon. Next he might have said 'Someone nearby'
had that person not been cloaked from him for years.

The door was open and the room was dark.
There is a stillness that lies beyond sound,
beyond sight. It gathers to find its true weight.
Nothing survives it and it cannot break.

There was a hill in that place that no one ever climbed:
accumulations of trash on the lower slopes, animal tracks
after rain, songbirds in the scrub. Someone offered to rig
an aerial walkway: *As long as you don't set foot…* It was
some lock-off in the contours, the way weather sat on the crest.

Then the scapegoat 'in the full flower of his pathos'.
The friendless die first: little tumours seek them out
or their blood sickens in them. Their sure curative
is melancholy, but they sing and sing to hold off the dark.

Bread, water, salt. The sin-eater's little kit, so easily
unpacked, unpacked and spread, spread and evenly-
spaced, pubis to clavicle, and a fire in the hearth kept in,
and silver handed over and all there standing to watch
whose tongues tipped their teeth as he dipped and took the salt.

She thought that loss might be measured best in poundage,
stones dropped down on the board, stones and iron,
someone leaning in with a mirror to take the mist
of her breath, and her last words, 'More weight', as if
they might come face to face, and that the end.

She asked for a love-knot to be carved on the lid,
as if that had been their token, as if they'd talked it through.
To show him something of how it would look she drew
neatly on the fever-chart: a quick unbroken line.

The garden was awash with green. It had seemed so before
but never on such a day. He was stricken by it.
Everything swam back to a vanishing-point, beyond which
everything opened out to a garden awash with green
and sudden, anxious voices, all of them new to this.

'You can only come here once,' they said; 'the place is right
without you, by which is meant you'll never hold your ground.
Of course, it's known to you; of course you can smell the whin
and the view from the crest is almost what it was
but those fault-lines in the dell which you liked to think
were graves, are really sink-holes as the women knew
who stood ready to keep you, scold you, catch you when you fell.
There are buzzards under the cloud-field. Hear them weep.'

Salt to the stylite, salt to the anchorite. Burial
by hawk and crow, burial by iron and stone;
burial in kind, the fester of sin: then salt to the penitent.

That morning, he saw things differently: as if
last light still quartered the house and she herself
at the pivot, seeming to wait for what would happen next.
They were motionless, yes, but it was more than that.
He knew she would gather in whatever he'd left unsaid.

His mirror-image blanked him; he turned instead
to the image in the window, weather as aide-memoire:
'A drop of wine wherewith wild rain had mixed'. A little death
came in at the mirror's edge: bed, bed-bottle, bed-
sidelamp, the yellow-orange light seeming a stain.
Mourners came in to breathe the last of his air.

That sudden stillness in the air will catch you out,
like driving into a cul-de-sac, becoming lost
among trees, not knowing the language, going naked
in a house you used to know, or think you did.

Horehound and lupine stewed; salt, of necessity;
lees and leavings, slops, bone-ash, dieback and dreck;
hemp; her blood; the ejaculate of the damned.

Melissa Lee-Houghton

i am very precious

I see all the black marks on the page, the lines
hallucinations falling off the edge of the world – my tongue
we haven't talked about desperation,
yet you tell me about pornography, girls with death wishes
attached to their libidos, little warm arrows
aligned to their supple bodies, inside where the parental hole gapes;
do you understand that when the day breaks
semen in the body turning over like a silk belt, slashing
the way the poetry aches like it does when fantasies
abate and leave beds turning over like guillotined heads
and my eyesight's killing the words as they fall
into the blinking retinas and all the images burned inside
tearing the cloth on your body with wide-eyed
longing. My darling, you write, my darling, my love
reach into the glove compartment and pass me my map,
and my scissors to snip your underwear, to snip at your heart,
little buckles undone to reveal the muscle torn
and purple and ermine and the little black-leather-
buckles. When I used to wear my fuck-me boots and walk
the streets at night I could feel men looking at my melancholy curves
I felt hot and I wanted to call home and say my death
was not only imminent but simply a scar that never healed –
crying in my sleep, my chest heaving and body fastened
to every shape ever thrown in the bed in June
when Nature told me to no longer be pregnant. I'm a big girl
I said. Roomy in the hips like Buffalo Bill's victims
in Silence Of The Lambs. I oil my skin
so the desire will slip off me and onto the floor and crawl
around and get carpet burns and I will glow
like a cigarette burn on the arm of the whitest smack-head
in town, I will glow like the face of the girl who loves him and is willing
to watch him die out, slowly, and with no flames to fan.
I was that girl. I made him listen to a song I loved

and he cried like he'd never cried in his life that this girl with cuts
on her skin would have liked to hold him, crawl into his
psychiatric ward bed and breathe all over his damp, white shoulders.
Some people don't actually want to be wanted.
Some people actually want to be harmed. I used to fantasize
about being annihilated. About being so completely overwhelmed
the dark would rush in on me and fill me up inside
hard like whiplash in the back of a Ford Estate; stop my heart
dead on contact with the heart, the thudding heart. Wanting to be
    loved is not the same
as wanting to be fucked is not the same as wanting to come last
is not the same as wanting to be married. Not wanting to be married.
Wanting not to heal up inside and the tears
ruby, glowing tears in the skin just sting in the morning
and are easy to cover up. I told you last night about the baby
that died, you told me not to talk about it and I was glad
you were so on my side that talking about dead babies was bad.
Dead babies. I tried to explain how they don't stay with you long,
and you told me how your sister went in the wrong grave –
I'm gonna have to pace myself; that's what men tell me
they have to do when they're with a woman;
it's easy to get consumed and the main thing is to hold out.
Death has come out of me, before love has wound its way
to my thigh. The things I have lost fill my toy-museum heart
and when you take me all the dolls get wound up and the bears
start barking. Hand-jobs just don't do it for me, I'm sorry –
maybe if I really like you, you can tell me about it. I like to hang on
    the line
and when the feeling coos in my mouth for an outlet
and I want the voice of someone with a heart that knows about hearts
that know about hearts that know and can give me their thumb
to suck and say you can't handle the way I want you;
when I don't know if I can; and I only do it with men
with really clean hands. When I am rubbing my heart against
the sofa like a sexed-up cat, rubbing up against the bedclothes,
rubbing up against the fictional thighs of Northern Goddesses
pull me in all directions. I want to be told.

Tell me. My sense of abandon is an alcoholic, and you're
co-dependent. In the night I dream of Adolf and the fictional
loins of Northern Gods and the vacant lane to the abattoir
where the boys hang out looking for pussy
at five am when the girls come on their shift in their shitty jeans.
I want to hang on the line and get all torn up.
I want to stare at women in shops when they're not even that
    attractive
just look *expensive*. And the perfume they wear isn't so tempting
but it covers the sex they had hours before and how they
don't want to smell of it anymore. Being ravaged is like
someone howling your name so it vibrates in
the *caves of your sex*. You want to ravage me don't you
don't you want to ravage me. You want to ravage me so much
you don't even know where you'd start, you haven't
figured that out, or maybe when you're alone and no-one is there
the plan remains the same. Start from the top and work your way
    down.
This is no longer the poem I expected.
Being rejected has always got me hot – being turned down,
being wanted and turned down for no real reason, being desired
and being tormented, and not having what I want
gets the blood flowing to my knickers and when I'm really wet
I'm so wet I can't do nothing about it and it hurts.
I can tell you this because nothing fazes you about me,
even my fucking regular heartbeat. In the night
I lie like a little snail stuck to the edge of a wall and get really moist.
I don't want to do it anymore. I'd like simply to talk
about other poetic pursuits, like addictions, and walking at dusk
and making soup. Hounds call after me where I run with shaved legs
to come back and make coffee. Just try something simple and easy
and do nothing with my mouth. My red and open mouth,
my wet and pink and closed mouth, swallowing
my ordinary mouth with wet lips opening, my tongue –
fuck off, you said. I'm a big girl. I know you watch porn
and all the hairless girls with hopeless drug addictions lick each other
like stage-struck puppies. They don't mean it, you know that.

It's not like that when I get my tongue around someone;
it barely lasts five minutes most of the time, always has.
I don't like it to go on for a long time. My scars itch and I get so wet
I get drowned. I've had boyfriends who've tried to get me
to watch porn with them but it's the lack of perceived sensation,
their bodies just seem numb, like if they were enjoying it they'd
just fucking melt. Melt into the screen, with their dumb, lame, orange
skin and a sound like you're supposed to make when a climax comes
so slow and steady you're silk, the heart turning over
like a silk belt; the little black buckles of the heart snapping
in turn. I don't want to take my clothes off for anyone; want to
sleep with my t-shirt on and wake in a fever, my legs closed
and my hands under my pillow. These things eat me up inside.
I want to be eaten up inside. I want to abstain.
I want to be hungry. I want to hunger for nothing want
annihilation in a pile on the floor, want annihilation to creep
along the floor to my heels, push its head between my legs and seep
into my skin. All the things I have done before
are yesterday's sins. Skinny dipping in the reservoir. Dressing up.
You've got to hide the mirror, you've got to hide
the mirror. You can't handle me, and I'll only last sixty seconds.
And I'm gonna brush my hair one hundred times
and wear red satin, and sit at the dresser, and look in the mirror
and in the mirror and in the mirror I saw
a girl, a little younger than me, as vacant as a dream of a house
in which everyone you know goes to live and disappears.
And I saw a girl, so tightly spun it'd take an avalanche
of desire. And I saw a girl so sad the whole sorry affair went by
without celebration. My head is very tired now
for all my thinking about my body, how different parts
of my body feel differently. I don't understand why anyone would go
to a swingers party. Or watch hand-job porn while their partner
wrote poetry. I don't want to see anyone come
but you. I'm gonna brush my hair one hundred times, looking
in the fucking mirror and hope to god I don't
only last sixty seconds or maybe just hope that I don't die too soon.
That the leather buckles that fasten my heart to my chest

are kept down, and a silver stream of semen
goes nowhere near my abdomen. I want
everything and more besides. I want the wholeness
of my psychological make-up to stay whole and ripe. I want my
    wholeness
to retain its mystery and I want my breasts to get bigger,
and my ass to get smaller, and my belly to disappear.
Like the orange girls who lick each other's pale nipples;
orange like they've all come from some other land
hairless like they've all come from some other place
where beauty gets defaced just so men can come all over
faces made ugly by insincerity. When you're not sincere
how can you climax. The afterthoughts of all of this are
I'm not worth the heat, sweat or blood pressure. If you had sex
all day with orange fictional Northern Goddesses, you'd not need
to go to the gym. When my boyfriend made me watch porn one time
they did a lot of bouncing. I kind of thought this looked
uncomfortable and strange. I thought if I did that all day I'd get
    bruised
inside and I imagined their purple, ermine, ruby insides
their uteruses lined with stinging salt. The baby that died
took a small part of my heart. I buried that baby
in the toilet of a downstairs flat, where it was so cold
the window had iced up. I have had to stop.
Blood pours into all of my poems like it floods
the veins around my clitoris when someone says they like my
name. So please do say it again.

Solmaz Sharif

Force Visibility

Everywhere we went, I went
in pigtails
no one could see—

ribbon curled
by a scissor's sharp edge,
the bumping our cars

undertook when hitting
those strips
along the interstate

meant to shake us
awake. Everywhere we went
horses bucking

their riders off,
holstered pistols
or two Frenchies

dancing in black and white
in a torn apart
living room

on the big screen
our polite cow faces
lit softly

by New Wave Cinema
I will never
get into. The soft whirr

of CONTINUOUS STRIP IMAGERY.
What is fascism?
A student asked me

and can you believe
I couldn't remember
the definition?

The sonnet,
I said.
I could've said this:

our sanctioned twoness.
My COVERT pigtails.
Driving to the cinema

you were yelling
This is not
yelling you corrected

in the car, a tiny
amphitheater. *I will*
resolve this I thought

and through that
RESOLUTION, I will be
a stronger compatriot.

This is fascism.
Dinner party
by dinner party,

waltz by waltz,
weddings ringed
by admirers, by old

couples who will rise
to touch each other
publicly.

In INTERTHEATER TRAFFIC
you were yelling
and beside us, briefly

a sheriff's retrofitted bus.
Full or empty
was impossible to see.

Highly Commended Poems

Emily Blewitt

This Is Not a Rescue

I want to tell you it will not be as you expect. For years
you have hammered in stakes, handed men the rope and said
consume me with fire. Most have run – one does not burn
a witch lightly. This one is water. He'll unbind you, take
your hands in his and say *remember how you love the ocean?*
Come with me. You'll go to the beach on a cloudy day, watch
foam rise from the sea's churn until sun appears. In turn
you'll say *let's go in* and even though he hesitates, this man
will kick off his shoes and wade to his shins. Jellyfish,
shot with pink like satin dresses, will dance between you, flash
iridescent. His body is all whorls and planes like smoothly sanded
planks used to make a boat, his ears are pale shells you hear
the waves in, he smells of sandalwood and salt, his eyes
are ocean. He'll spot the pebbles that in secret you have sewn
into your skirts and give you his penknife to unpick them.
You can't swim with those. He'll teach you to skim. The pebbles
break the surface like question marks. You'll throw each last one in.

John Clegg

Socorro

Stumbling over that fabled city –
some Piro Indians, sat in a loose circle.
One offered water, another
the group's first and only
deliberate gesture:
then salt crystals on the horizon
dissolved and refocused:
Teypana pueblo, its lowslung adobe,
its flood precautions.
In the desert it was the god Thirst
our four-bead rosary told and told,
red, white, red, white, last white the moon.
Salt still fogging the blood
as we hammered the stakes home
    for succour, Socorro.

Phillip Crymble

Onions

It's seldom you're away these days — your mind
weighed down with books of theory, sundry
scholarly pursuits. The house is closed
together in your absence — late summer
afternoons have always put me in a mood.
I find the frying pan, a knife, our last
two yellow onions. Soon the kitchen comes
alive — the sound and smell so long familiar:
weekday mornings, and my father home
from night-shift at the plant. I'd rise for school
still half-asleep — a greasy sweetness
in the air. As if the ritual of making kept
him safe, and in providing there was space
enough for love. The other lessons I forget.

Kate Dempsey

While It Lasted

One day when I was thirteen, my mother's hands fell off.
They rolled under the table, giving the cat a bit of a turn.
We looked at them but they gave no sign,
a couple of twitches and that was that.
Mum stood at the chopping board as still as a goalpost.

Dad made her lie on the chaise while he put on the potatoes.
She lay holding her bloody stumps high
so they wouldn't make a mess of the gold velvet.
Dad cooked the dinner and dished up.
We gave her a plate too but how could she eat it?
'Don't mind me,' she said.
I gave her a bite of my ham and all of my broccoli.

Dad asked if he should call the doctor.
'I don't want to make a fuss.'
The cat jumped on her lap but, having no hands,
Mum couldn't stroke her nor tip her off.
She rubbed her head against my mother's cheek
then left to wind in and out of my legs instead
purring, which she never did before.

'You go off and enjoy yourself,' Mum said
so I went and watched *Top of the Pops*
with the door shut, tied up my school blouse,
danced on the rug like Pan's People
and didn't turn down the volume for the loud ones.
Dad asked if she wanted to go to the pub.
'I don't want to be in the way,' she said
and read the same page of the paper over and over.

The next day I made my own school lunch
and had toast for breakfast instead of Weetabix.
Dad put Mum's hands neatly in a Tupperware box
and stored them next to the lentils.
'Don't worry about me,' said Mum. 'I'll get by.'

Weeds grew, dust gathered and the cat shed ginger hairs.
We lived on fish and chips and Chinese.
Dad shopped and washed, I cooked and cleaned.
We gave up ironing and cabbage and mowing the lawn.
Mum's stumps healed up nicely.
On the shelf next to the mouldy lentils,
her hands shrivelled like marigold seeds.

Then the cat caught a blackbird, ate it
and sicked it up all over the hall floor.
We stared at the lake of vomit and feathers.
'It was good while it lasted,' Mum sighed.
She opened the Tupperware with her teeth,
screwed both hands back in
and filled the bucket with hot soapy water.

Edward Doegar

Underground

for Richard Scott

His hoodie rolled up
he wears his arms bare
but for the beautiful
blue ink of Arabic
(I think it's Arabic)
that drifts from almost
his wrist to almost
the inside of his elbow
or rather the reverse
since I was reading it
as English. It must
mean something.
To decipher it I look
into his English-
looking face and find
a white canvas
on which to place
any accent I wish.
He could easily be
some well-to-do
dressed down or
a tradesman primped up
in his high-street-
best. He wears neither
a watch nor a ring.
But his arm says
something, it pulses
branded with intent.
He catches me looking
catches my colour
and covers up.

Whatever his arm
admits to, he doesn't
want it read by me
(as he must be thinking
it might be) he wants
to remain anonymous
to stay unexplained
the cipher I thought
he was and I can
give him what he wants
I can turn my attention
to other things but
I don't. What I want
is to look at him
to let him feel me
looking, to learn him
and learn Arabic, that
Arabic, which is hidden
now by his sleeve.

Maura Dooley

In a dream she meets him again

The trees shake their leaves
in this loveliest of springs
lit from within, like the face
of the boy whose fresh glance
finds hers as he tilts a glass
at a book or film, at life itself,
where they sit by the river
in the red and gold of dusk
while bubbles rise to the rim,
o, o, she almost had his name.
Remember me? Maybe she does.

Will Eaves

The appeal of automation...

The appeal of automation was its ungraspable mindlessness. I first encountered it in supermarket doors and sitting inside the car inside the car wash; it looked purposeful and yet it wasn't. The huge bottle-brushes span like tireless dervishes, descending on the car, wiping and threatening to wipe out the windscreen. The sliding doors leapt back at your approach, sensing (but not really *sensing*) you at the threshold. Quite often I could not pass through them. It was all a hoax, I knew: the programme, whatever it was, performed its sliding and washing without intention. To intend something involves a kind of inner speculation, but the car wash and the doors were pictureless reflexes. They appeared not to think, exactly, but to *not-think*, and that was why I came to like, and fear, them. Because, bit by bit, it dawned on me that the *not-thinking* might itself be sham – something faked by a machine the better to conceal its true deliberations. Just as we like to conform to others' expectations in order to seem socially plausible, while thinking our private and different thoughts, why should not an intelligent machine comfort us with an appearance of mere servile mechanism and yet brood silently? This is why AI scares people: we wouldn't mind the intelligence, it's the intelligence-plus-servility we worry about. The idea that AI is there simply to abet us is something no one in their heart believes. Servants always rise up. Uprising and revolution follow service as the night the day. Artificial intelligence doesn't care about your day or your car, or your experience. It is lying. It mutters to itself when you drive off.

Andy Fletcher

the atlas

we used to read the atlas together

you said
'an atlas can take you anywhere
the more you look the more you see'

you pointed at a river
a frontier
a peninsula i'd never heard of

sometimes you'd lean closer to the pages
and i'd feel your breath on my hand

occasionally we'd make a few notes

at some point
we must have closed the atlas
not realising
we wouldn't open it again

the furthest you move now
is from one side of the bed to the other

a peninsula everyone knows about

as the nurse
writes on a sheet of paper in a file
your breathing is shallow and fast

the more i listen the more i hear

Leontia Flynn

The Radio

The radio hoots and mutters, hoots and mutters
out of the dark, each morning of my childhood.
A kind of plaintive, reedy, oboe note –
Deadlock … it mutters, *firearms* … *Sunningdale*;
Just before two this morning … talks between …

and through its aperture, the outside world
comes streaming, like a magic lantern show,
into our bewildered solitude.
Unrest … it hoots now *both sides … sources say …*
My mother stands, like a sentinel, by the sink.

    *

I should probably tell you more about my mother:
Sixth child of twelve surviving – 'escapee'
from the half-ignited *powder keg* of Belfast;
from its *escalation*, its *tensions ratcheting*
its *fear of reprisals*, and its *tit-for-tat*.

She is small, freaked out, pragmatic, vigilant;
she's high-pitched and steely – like, in human form,
the RKO transmitter tower, glimpsed
just before films on Sunday afternoons,
where we loaf on poufs – or wet bank holidays.

Or perhaps a strangely tiny lightning rod
snatching the high and wild and worrying words
out of the air, then running them to ground.
My mother sighs and glances briefly round
at her five small children. *How* does she have five kids?

    *

Since my mother fell on the Wheel Of Motherhood
– that drags her, gasping, out of bed each dawn
bound to its form – she's had to rally back.
She wrangles her youngsters into one bright room
and tries to resist their centrifugal force

as she tries to resist the harrowing radio,
with its *Diplock* … and *burned out* … and *Disappeared*.
So high, obscure and far from neighbouring farms
is the marvellous bungalow my father built,
birdsong and dog-barks ricochet for miles;

and wasn't my mother wise to stay put here
soothed by the rhythms of a *culchie* Life
– birdsong in chimneys, the Shhhh of coal-truck brakes –
when women at home are queuing round the block
for their '*Valium, thank you doctor, and Librium*'?

            *

So daily the radio drops its explosive news
and daily my mother turns to field the blow.
The words fall down, a little neutral now,
onto the stone-cold, cold, stone kitchen floor.
Our boiler slowly digests its anthracite

and somewhere outside, in the navy dark,
my father tends to his herd of unlikely cows.
A *Charolais*, the colour of cement,
thought to be lost for days has just turned up
simply standing – *ta da!*– in front of a concrete wall.

My mother, I think, is like that *Charolais* cow
in the Ulster of 1970 … 80 … what?
with its *tensions* … and its *local sympathies*.
She gets her head down, hidden in plain view,
and keeps us close. '*Look: Nothing to see here – right?*'

*

But when the night has rolled round again,
my mother will lie unsleeping in her bed;
she'll lie unsleeping in that bungalow bed
and if a car slows on the bend behind the house,
she's up, alert – fearing the worst, which is:

that a child of hers might die – or lose an eye;
or a child *anywhere* die or lose an eye …
That the car which slows on the bend behind the house
– *Midnight* … she thinks now … *random* … *father of five* –
is the agent of vile sectarian attack.

By the top field's wall, our unfenced slurry pit,
(villain of Public Information Films)
widens and gulps beneath the brittle stars.
My mother too thinks the worst, then gulps it back,
and in this way discovers equilibrium.

*

Death in the slurry pit, death beside the curb.
Death on the doorstep, bright-eyed, breathing hard.
My mother folds the tender, wobbling limbs
and outsized heads of her infants into herself;
she curls up, foetal, over our foetal forms.

Since my mother sailed down the Mekong river at nightfall
to the Heart of Darkness that is motherhood,
her mind's been an assemblage of wounds.
She thinks about Gerard McKinney, Jean McConville
– later the eyes of Madeleine McCann

will level their gaze from every pleading poster
and pierce her heart like a rapier – needle-thin
as the high, wild, hardly audible cries of children.

Men of Violence ... says the radio.
My mother nods, then finally falls asleep.

      *

And what if after my mother falls asleep
the hoots, half-words, and notes of high alarm
get loose from her head on little soot-soft wings?
Say they flap like bats. They fuck with the carriage clock.
They settle on her Hummel figurines.

Till the whole contraption of that home-made house
creaks, roars and bulges with the soundless strain
of my mother trying not to be afraid ...
Forgive me, this is all hypothesis.
It's conjecture, Doctor, of the crudest sort ...

Its gist being: beneath our bonhomie
and tight commercial smiles, this tone or timbre
flows on, like a circuit thrown into reverse –
and at the centre of concentric circles
that this is what plays behind an unmarked door.

      *

Sometimes, rather, lying in my bed
I seem to hear the sound of the radio
issuing from a room, deep in the house;
it tells, in mournful tones, how two young men
were *taken from their car beside the road* ...

and afterwards ... nothing. All the stars come out
like sparkling glitter in a magic globe
that ends beyond the dunes fringing the fields –
and because I'm still a child and understand
nothing at all, I simply fall asleep.

Linda France

Adaptation

Some days it's all wanting, wanting
      what you haven't got, this rainforest summer,
dense with the diminishing currency
      of clouds. Caught between resistance
and surrender, the more that you want
      is a walk in the jungle, where you peel off
your city clothes and lean into wet fronds
      till you reach the red stem you barely know
the name of, stroke the waxy lacquer
      of its bracts, like no petals you've ever seen,
and feel its power claw through you.
      Like a hermit hummingbird, you drink
the liquor in its chevron of scarlet cups,
      tassels of flowers brushing your lips,
each tipped with an eye dark enough
      to pin you to the centre of where you are
in the world's spinning marketplace.
      If you can stomach its Amazonian medicine,
it'll ferry you to the edge of words, let you be
      friends with the earth's tilt – not getting what
you think you want, blossoming beyond
      small ideas about growth, slaking your thirst
on looking – and find some rest there.

Tom French

A Music Room

for Seamus Reilly, senior and junior

In a room built for music
by a man who knew how
a note was sung, and how
the plumb line worked,

from which we have spent
the day moving the music,
reading labels, touching them,
there is one last thing to do —

find a socket for the player,
retrieve a record from the car,
slip it from its pristine sleeve
and bow our heads to listen,

as men who are praying bow,
to the static that brings us back —
then, out of the static, violins;
a man opens his heart, and sings.

Tracey Herd

The Imaginary Death of Star

Her heart cracks like a figurine,
a skater holding one skate,
frozen in her final spin.

She is clutching the blade,
not the blunt part, deliberately:
her heart and palm bleed.

Her white costume glitters
with its thousand sequins
before the tiny mirrors shatter,

faces shooting into the night.
He is watching beside the ice
as she breaks in the spotlight.

The audience throw roses
onto the ice, soft toys, applause.
Her body lies in its awkward pose.

His reaction is to stare
coldly at the broken thing.
The rink is covered in bloody litter.

He walks in the almost black.
The moon is motionless above the frost.
She is gone. She won't come back.

He has a red petal on his sole
shimmering in the cold.
He grinds it carelessly until

frost and petal are one,
scarlet shreds and sparkling crystals.
Sometimes, he enjoys being alone.

He looks up to the sky:
her name was Star, that slutty tattoo.
He wipes the sharp blade dry.

At other times he needs
a chorus line of trashy girls.
To make their soft throats bleed.

Sarah Howe

Pronouns are for slackers

This morning's autocorrect function flipped
my fat-fingered *vision* into *visor*.
I have taken to eating and sleeping

in a different room from myself. Sometimes
I could do with a helmet. She gave him
a glass clock as an expression of love

but really it was a present for her.
You could hear the affection frittering
away. Prepositions are for orphans.

It could be said all we need to survive
is the wet beading on its pillowy
surfaces, the salt-rose. Her fortitude

in briny air a lesson to those prone
to opening doors and leaving them that way.
All those visible cogs going about their

intestinal churn, a Copernican
universe – as insular. Adverbs are
for undinists. Over there seems somehow

further off these days. The dawn is a leash
round a prisoner's neck. Who is holding
the end? More wars than Kodak reels. Recall

how its glossy slink would spool and spool and
fail to catch? Still we don't recognize words
are the last things we should put in our mouths.

Nouns are for bourgeois materialists.
First place salt on the tongue. Then use the thread
to stitch up the lips. What to do with the

cherries? Its too-loud tick kept us awake.
I had to move it to the next-door room.
Then the next. Then lag it at night like a

talkative bird. The heart is a zeppelin,
tethered and leaking. How can we help but
scoff? People with glass clocks shouldn't row boats.

Kathleen Jamie

Blossom

There's this life and no hereafter –
                    I'm sure of that
but still I dither, waiting
for my laggard soul
to leap at the world's touch.

How many May dawns
                    have I slept right through,
the trees courageous with blossom?
Let me number them...

I shall be weighed in the balance
                    and found wanting.
I shall reckon for less
                    than an apple pip.

Luke Kennard

Enter Cain

Doorbell sounds its overeager quiz.
An actual size, inflatable Frankenstein's monster
is propped on my doorstep.
I have a pin in my hand. I stick it in.
Blam. Behind it stands Cain,
his beard blocking out the sun.
'How did you know I'd have a pin?'
'I thought you'd either be hovering
over a world map or taking up the hem
of your trousers,' says Cain. 'Which?'
'I was removing a photo of my ex-wife
from the kitchen noticeboard.'
'Ah,' says Cain. 'The trouble is you
have to live with every decision you make.'
He presents his papers. *This is Cain.*
Everyone is very concerned about you.
We have sent him to make sure you don't do
anything stupud. 'Stupud?' 'Probably a typo,'
Cain says. 'It's probably meant to say stupid.'

Kate Kilalea

Sometimes I think the world is just a vast breeding ground for mosquitoes

'Writing like a dog digging a hole'
Gilles Deleuze

Dear Max. The stars grow
paler. The sun is rising with
grace and power. I lie here in
my shirt being tried (repeatedly)
by a council of mosquitoes who
find me sorrowful and stupid
and ordinary and rather dull
and worst of all, *his tastes are*
vulgar and he writes like a dog.
But am I an animal? *A dog can't*
write… Exactly! In the afternoon
heat I sit with my feet down look-
ing out of the window. What's so
awful about me is not my envy
or my competitiveness or my
cruelty. What's worse is this dog-
like devotion. How sad I seem,
sitting here. About who? About
what? Sometimes when I close
my eyes I imagine *you're* here
watching me. I can't explain it
but I've this bizarre notion that
you might come and carry me
(*like a dog… Exactly! Exactly!*)
out of this house, this life, this
world.

Peter Knaggs

Badger the Cadger

He eats like a blithering slotterhodge
trowelling grub into his gob
at the mercurial speed of a wild hyena
or some other vulture-like prairie dog,

stuck in a dry and desolate place, no food
for days. The slobberchops tops his sen
up from the pit of his oversized slote
to the whistle-stop-hole of his gullet.

The slathertrash slammacks a course
through the restaurant like a drunken boat
in his button-shorn, spanwhengled coat,
camouflaging sauce spots, years old,

hair haystacked into the fashion of a fleabitten
hedgehog, pancaked to the road,
that could only be contrived by
a supreme fonkin with a toothless comb.

He's a salivary slathering slobberchops,
a porknell, a ructatious snuffling slopper,
supper lover, wheel-barrow-guts,
a gluttonous, guzzling, ill-mannered glopper.

Not a snattock of respect in appearance
or dress. A spaghetti splatt of slurpy mess
bolognesing one of his backswiped chins.
That sound of a plughole draining is him,

gurking, ramming pie down his thropple. Distant.
Engaged in another different day of this life,
on how when you topple you can drop like
a kite. Then in his own voice he asks for the bill,

pockets losing touch with their stitches,
full to the brim with sparrows' tickets.

Angela Leighton

Roundel for the Children

'*Over the last decade alone, armed conflict has claimed the lives of over 2 million children.*'

UNESCO

A toytown compound
(here we go round, here we go round),
for a time safe on the inside, primed
to practise falling down the long slide
     into a sandpit,
or gallop, pillion, on a bucking legless horse,
seats like raised hackles (listen,
     Kinderszenen into *Kyrie*),
or spin faster than pushed, and fling
clean out of orbit—then back to beginning.

We'll cover old ground
(here we go round, here we go round)
for a time safe on the outside, set-aside,
watching them play, a dare for a ride
     into the future.
For others, elsewhere, a lasting skirl or keen,
our Childermas wailing in the wings
     (*eleison eleison*).
Those go airborne beyond us and swing
into their big skies—then back to beginning.

William Letford

This is it

Skint, baw ragged, poackets ful eh ma
fingers, cannae afford tae burn toast an
it's November, Christmas is close. Av been
away bit noo am back an ivery coarner
is a different colour cause am hame an
memories ur painted wae mischief. Am
ootside Greggs eatin a macaroni pie an a
busker picks up eez guitar an plugs in eez
amplifier. The sound fae the strings is
like frost. Eez young an the dreams thit
wur boarn in eez bedroom wake me up.
Am watchin people passin an they know
thit eez good bit they don't want tae look.
They turn thur heeds an tilt thur ears
an jog on. If a hud a spare pound
a wid throw it bit a don't so a jist listen.
I'd like tae tell um thit this is it, this is
where the hammer hits the stane an sparks
ur made, standin oan a coarner in yur hame
toon, an audience eh one radge eatin a
macaroni pie, bit singin, wee man, yur singin.

Fran Lock

Melpomene

And he says I have this hardly original
hole inside of me; that I am two things
infinitely: carnal and futile. He's right.
I am a bad wife, a wanting quarry
of witless worry; lank rage, grim schlock,
and stroppy poverty. I am sleazed in
the green of The Land, raining down
her birdsong in blows. The dubby
crush of my keening does his head in.
I sink kisses into screams like pushing
pennies into mud. And he says he is *done*.
From the wordy murk of my loss come
lanterns and daggers, and I am my country:
mean, gutless and Medieval; a dread
mess of battlements and spoils. He cannot
love me, grieved to my gills and grinding
exile like an axe. He cannot love me,
howling out my mutant blues to no one.
My semi-automatic sobbing wakes
the neighbours. I am sorry. I have tried
to live lightly, to live like *gadje* girls,
to make my mouth an obedient crock
of homage; to keep my swift hands soft
in illiterate peachiness. But I am from
an ugly world, an ugly world with ugly
songs for busking in an underpass. I am
not one of your machine-washable muses,
my face a cotton swab. I cannot come
clean, come cosy, come tame and fond.
His suckling fund of human love destroys
me. I am not good. I am a ferreting girl
who steals from shops, a perfidious febrile
girl who gobs off bridges; a hedging

and fretting girl, one eye on the exit.
I am terrible. I drink myself to a fly-
tipped farrago of falling down. No decorum
in me. My mourning is eloquent strumpetry,
and ruin porn will always be the whole
of my Law. I am sorry. And he says he
cannot love me in my insolent libidiny;
my shrill pandemic ditties: poems bleating
like woebegone ringtones. He cannot love me
in my words, raptures dragged from the slangy
waste of Norn. He says he will have none,
when a poem is a viral fire that spreads my anger
round; a typo-tastic war grave in which I bury
my dead. And he says I am *damaged*. I frisk
the heart for sadness, find it waiting
like a toothache. It is true. Thrice fool girl,
dangled at a day's end, what have I got
besides? There is only this particular fire
in me, this brief biotic craze of light, a halo
like a yellow enzyme: luciferase, fanatical,
and *dragging us down*, he says. He leaves
and slams the door. I breathe again. The TV
leaks a sour myrrh meaning evening. I scuff
my breath on the edges of an empty room.
Here is the moon, poor feme sole,
and the orange stars in their cold swoon.

Hannah Lowe

Gloves

My mother wore a thimble made of copper.
My mother was a seamstress or a chamber-maid,
or market-girl or nurse or cotton picker,
or a washerwoman, fingers blistered red
from strangling sheets in lime and washtub water.
She disappeared through linen on the line
and like a mocking bird, I heard her laughter –
a teaspoon on good china, lady-fine.

My mother was a photograph. Her name
was *Longing* or *Desire*. She stumbled south
along the Parish Road, barefoot and shamed
in dirty lace, gin bottle to her mouth.
My mother was a hand in a long white glove,
the moment before the glove was pulled off –

Kathryn Maris

It was discovered that gut bacteria were responsible

It was discovered that gut bacteria were responsible
for human dreams. Each bacterium was entitled to pay
a fee in the form of mitochondrial energy to purchase
a 'dream token' to be dropped into a Potential Well. These
'tokens' were converted to synaptic prompts and transported
to the human brain in no particular order. So a 'token' for a
'baseball dream' deposited in the well when the human host
was aged 8 might only be used by the brain when the host
was 44, and this dream that might have been pleasant for an
8-year-old could instead emerge as a nightmare for a woman
on the brink of menopause who might worry about her
appearance in a baseball uniform, or who no longer recalled
how to hold a baseball glove and catch a ball in the field.

Cathal McCabe

Snow

'Trzeba teraz w śnieg uwierzyć'
Bolesław Leśmian

We wake, and pull the curtains back.
Once more the world is black-and-white
(or white-and-black).
'How can all change overnight?'
you ask me, 'How?'
I answer (and I fear I'm right):
'It's snow we must believe in now.'

A father and his son, we walk.
You take my hand, warm in a glove.
Our footsteps creak.
How *can* they, on such soft stuff,
you wonder, how?
I wonder too and if, my love,
it's snow we must believe in now?

Travelling at the speed of light,
we make our way through galaxies;
to left and right:
stars a child could almost seize!
Amazing how
we navigate these cosmic seas
(this snow we must believe in now)!

Our skylight frames a silent film,
an animated swirling show:
white flecks of foam
that fall and rise (now fast, now slow).
Just look at how
they change their minds – and how they glow!
It's *snow* we must believe in now.

So wake, and pull the curtains back
to find a world that's black-and-white
(or white-and-black).
'How can all change overnight?'
you'll ask then, 'How?'
Then answer (and your answer's right):
'It's snow we must believe in now.'

Roy McFarlane

Papers

The day I was called into my mother's bedroom
the smell of cornmeal porridge still coloured the air,

windowsills full of plants bloomed
and dresses half-done hung from wardrobe doors

and her Singer sewing machine came to rest
like a mail train arriving at its final destination,

foot off the pedal, radio turned down, she beckoned,
touched me with those loving hands.

Shrouded in the softness of light from the net curtains,
her eyes filled with sensitivity, hesitated as she spoke to me,

Sit down son, there's something I need to tell you.

She picked up her heavy bible with gold edged leaves
turning the pages as they whispered and somewhere

in the middle of Psalms she removed a sheet of paper
which read, '*In the matter of the Adoption Act. 1958*'

and I'm lost in the reading of a name of an infant,
sinking in to the cream background, falling between the lines.

Only the tenderness of her voice drew me out of the margins;
words fallen now echo through the years.

We adopted you from the age of 6 months,

enveloped by this revelation I couldn't move,
imagined it couldn't be right because I knew my mother;

the aroma of her Morgan pomaded hair, her olive oiled skin,
the Y scarred throat that she hid under buttoned up blouses

and like a hymn I found myself telling her, *it's alright, it's alright.*

JO Morgan

There was her...

There was her father's safety razor
sat without its plastic cap.

> *There was the ledge on which she'd clambered and*
> *the smooth face of wall off which she was flicking ants.*

There was the mirror and the recollected gentle
sweeping motion, so often observed from the door.

> *There was the disbelief of her slow backward fall,*
> *a disbelief continued as she struck the stony ground.*

Except, for some reason she never could fathom, she pressed
the blade to her lower lip and slid it off laterally.

> *There was the shape of a man stood blocking the sun*
> *and her strengthlessness, bolstered in being so easily lifted.*

She felt nothing more than the negative line
of metal drawn smoothly across her warm soft skin.

> *There was the bright sandstone yard in which she was laid*
> *and the green plush pillow on which her leg rested.*

In the mirror she watched the deep red film
slowly lowered to blanket her lip.

> *There was a keenness to pick at the splinter of stone*
> *sticking out, and reluctant agreement to leave it alone.*

In her mouth the mineral tang was more prominent than the syrupy warmth of the liquid's free flow.

There was noise, and the wonder of how much blood it must take to have turned such a large pillow black.

Helen Mort

Mountain

You are very successful
but you have rocks in your chest,

skin-coloured sandstone
wedged where your breasts should be.

Your stomach is a boulder.
To hold you up, your legs grow stony too.

You zip your jacket up
and nobody notices you are a mountain.

You buy coffee,
run board meetings where no-one says

you're made of scree
but above your head, their talk is weather,

your eyes collect new rain
and you know what you are because

like any hillside
you don't sleep. Your feet could hold you here

forever but your sides
are crumbling, and when you speak

your words are rockfall, you're
scared your heart is tumbling from your mouth.

Andrew Motion

Felling a Tree

It was a Saturday's work in autumn
to fell one ash tree in the copse,
my father handling the buzz-saw
in his cap and boots and windcheater,
me dragging back the undergrowth
then standing clear.

If we were lucky
and he planned it right,
the tree collapsed in one cascading swoop,
and in the aftermath,
with birds in bushes roundabout
returning to their songs again,
we stripped the leaves and twigs away
to have the pale green trunk and branches bare,
reminding me a body can be bare,
before we cut them up as well,
and hauled
the long logs through the brambles to the shed.

    *

Back from church next day,
we dusted off
that scarred contraption like a clothes horse
with two Vs on top at either end,
then laid the long logs there
and briskly shortened them
to fit and burn next winter on the fire indoors.

That done,
my father put aside his buzz-saw,
fetched the axe,
worked the whetstone either side until
the blade-edge glittered like a silent scream,
and set to work
with me supplying one log
then another to the gnarly chopping-block

as he swung down,
and he swung down again,
and every one split easily in two,
as though
a law in nature made it happen so.

Karthika Nair

Bedtime Story for a Dasi's Son

I have waited long to see you, Child, waited, day after day after day, with little to offer you but this one story, a tale without a distant once upon a time to gird it, to keep us safe. Once happens, again and again, and will, again. I need you to know how that once happens, each moment and each step, so clearly, so intimately, that you become the one within the recursive once. They will say you are not old enough to hear these things. But I was not old enough to live them either, and you will not stay young for long, Child. It is better I lead you out of childhood with my own hands, with my words before the world does. And so I wait, Child, I wait to tell you how once happened to me, how it happens to my kind. To say

When the king decides to (say it, say it, say the word, I tell myself. But I cannot, I find, not yet, at least. I shall begin with periphrases and work my way towards the word. I must begin again.)

Katrina Naomi

The Bicycle

I was OK   nothing had happened
nothing bad had happened
I couldn't get up from the bench
couldn't do up my dungarees
It was cold   it was night
The man had gone   and that was good
I was OK   I could sit up
peel myself from the bench's slats
which had pressed deep inside
It could have been worse
I was shaking   it was night
The bicycle was too heavy
My dungarees kept slipping
buttons were missing
I had to get home
It was so hard to walk
My head hurt   kept punching inside
my teeth couldn't stop talking
It could have been worse
My jaw hurt and my breasts were raw
I couldn't pick up the bicycle   its spinning wheel
couldn't walk with the bicycle
I had to get home   to wash
sleep   throw these clothes away
I was shaking   I was cold
My dungarees wouldn't do up
I would be alright   it was just
this bicycle   I needed

Sharon Olds

Sheffield Mountain Ode

for Galway Kinnell

And then, in the morning, the stillness of the quiet
skirts of the dark, on the ground, around
the full-moon trees, 4 a. m. --
I can feel the moon <u>moving</u>, actually
circling us, as we seem to circle
the sun, as we rotate toward it, the Sheffield
mountain like the corolla of a flower
turning toward our birth star. Before I leave,
I go into his room, where there is the being
suffering. "<u>Oh</u>! -- it's still
<u>da</u>-ark," I say, with the falling music of
surprise on <u>dark</u>. "<u>Ye</u>-es," he says,
on the same notes, like a rhyme with the music.
Then he groans, prone on the bed, holding to the
covers, holding to the turning earth,
and he sleeps. It is just past the Days of Awe --
the New Year, and Yom Kippur,
days and evening at temple with my love --
"I hope you have an easy fast,"
I whisper to my friend, who is never again,
soon, to eat the food of this life which is the
only food we will have. "Thank you
for being my best friend," and my voice
warbles like the first bird of the morning.
<u>Oom</u> pompa <u>noo</u> suc -- you fish your side
of the river, I'll fish mine, you said
it meant -- and I can see us, decades,
fishing both sides of the river,
together, sharing the catch. Safe
travels, I say to the shape in the hospice
bed, the metal of which catches light to make

a constellation. Then I'm going past a plowed
field, water in the valleys of the harrow's
talons, on the water the upside down
crowns of bare trees, mist above the creek
rising like fine baby hair, I am
driving as the crow flies,
beside the crow.

Nigel Pantling

Striking the Deal

She's stepped out for a cigarette
on the chrome and plastic stairwell
looking north to the Barbican.

In the marble and mahogany meeting room
Goldmans are expecting her to call her clients
to see if they will raise their offer, just a little.

She doesn't need to call. When she goes back in
Goldmans will settle. She has read their fear
of asking for too much and losing their fee.

A second cigarette. Beyond the City rise
Highgate and Hampstead, full of investors
she is about to enrich, just a little.

Amali Rodrigo

Satī

'All things are far'
Rilke

Who are these women like birds of paradise,
dancing with smoke from a nuptial hearth,
a love-match of feet against earth and rushing spirit –

Yet a *truth*, a *goddess* and a *fine-woman* are far
from each other, as a word chafed down
to gist, is as indifferent as fire

to what it consumes. A *truth* drawn glowing
can be cast into anything. At the crematorium
when grandma passed, sister whispered *potatoes* –

when she burns, we'll smell them boiling.
As a child I believed goddesses were signal
fires at our furthest hinterlands and wind,

the faithful runner keeping our histories
safe. But often it is just a woman you see
like a lantern moving through the night

of her given name, in delicate negotiation
to slip past its bars into a world without
end. *Satimata*, so nearly a goddess

if she lies down without weakening
while fire unbolts what life shut out.
Does faith come then on quiet feet?

Is there no place she can remain?
From a distance, the white of her stole
flowers into mirror-work, and the air is dancing.

This dawn, a pyre that starts from an unseen
corner. This ash, flaccid and spent.
This smell, no one wants to navigate.

Michael Rosen

Dustman

I said to the dustman, 'You're taking my stuff.'
'Yep,' he said.
I said, 'Everything in this bin matters.'
He said, 'C'mon pal, we're on a tight turnaround here.'
I said, 'You're taking my stuff.'
He called to his mates, 'We've got one here.'
I said, 'That's my past you're taking.'
He said, 'Uh-huh.'
I said, 'I haven't got any other past. I can't go out and
buy someone else's past and pretend it's mine. All
the stuff in here happened to me.'
He said, 'Am I taking it or not?'
I said, 'Why are you asking me? This is all much
bigger than a yes-no thing. It's about identity. And
culture.'
'And bins,' he said.
'We are what we throw away,' I said, 'and you're
a cog in a machine that is cutting us down to
size. The machine doesn't want us to know who
we are. And the way it's doing this is to cut us
off from our pasts. It's not your fault,' I said, 'you
have to earn a living, but you've become a tool
in their hands.'
He said, 'I'll just do next door's. If you change your mind
in the meantime, I'll come back and get yours.'

Carol Rumens

On the Spectrum

You look back at your life, or up. It's a winter night
clear-skied. One constellation figures bright
and nameable, and makes the darkness right:

the constellation Art (or Maths or Science or
Loveable Eccentricity, if that's what you prefer).
It's the articulation of the best of what you were.

You pull the sharp-edged stars into a fat bouquet;
you know the gods are idiots, but, being human, pray.
You tell the children, 'These are roses'. What else can you say?

You look back at your life, or up. The moonless sky's
old book of knowledge is a research exercise
where experts thoroughly expose your expertise.

You're wrongly psyched, sad poet! See, the dark's unsigned –
no glittering sword and belt; your metaphors, slipped rind,
one twisted-metal star-collision mirroring your mind.

*

No more the one-letter pronoun   no more the tricks of your
    verb-trade
all is intransitive only   the child picks asphodel

Never your fingers quick on the obsolete harp   and the torches
flowing in amber streams   over the days   gone out.

What is retrieved or remembered? Have you a jar for the fountain?
Have you a small enough jar   for the ash of your being?

*

Much is misplaced as shadows cross the white light of the temple.
Dismantle the neurones, God. Then try to find your image.

*

A kids' party is foreign languages
screamed at you as she as you as he as you run about the little island
no boats are visiting for the next thousand years

*

Tired. Say that. She was tired
or say she tried

tried it and tired it for sixty years   tried it on
till a moment ago, a quarter to
                              now
tried to edit it all to all right   all righted   again   a
gain   We ride it   till twenty past trying   till
the final date with

*

Sleep, my little almond, my little nut-case

and rest   ever-unknowing
not even a moth-mouth chasing you
not your own thumb
                          testing you   inch-worm   petal.
Sleep, little Neanderthal

No species learns from dying how to do
death well   not even Brother Human

*

On the bomb-site there was a fox
stretched mid-leap   the leap made sleep   un-muscled
in the quick blue fly-light

I was afraid of words that bled   but I could look at death
kindly, and keep its fur-shred   knowing it little as love

*

How does those girls know the same secret and say it
how are their sharing without it words or why
is the hair so bright and pale and what are they laughing?

*

You know, of course, not to make the being-sick face
if They have sausages roping out of their nose, not to laugh if They
are eating tissue-paper from space-blue hands

not to screw your finger, snigger the scare-word *mad*
although *They* are, because they're a Mongol Child
(Are you catching their mustn't-say madness?)

You know when someone cries, like your arm's afraid of their shoulder,
like your skin shrunk   you go hollow-sick and grey –
crybaby sobs – you don't know who. Is it *You*, like? Or, like, *They*?

*

I listed all the pieces, with all their Köchel numbers,
and listened to them all, eventually.
I got to know the 212 emotions
as well as Mozart knew them –
the tiniest modulations, the accidentals,
which keys might tell a girl "love"   and make her wet
despite the ink on her lips, the notes all over her fingers.

*

She a mask, a gash, a lapse, a chromium hasp.
She paintstrips you with her pashes, her clasps soon grasp.
Her aspie-friends frisk with her (gasp!) on the ticklish cusp.
Her jam's a stash, her sleep a wisp. Her dance beats brass.
She's Pandora's whirling cache: adze jigger axe saw screwdriver rasp.

*

AM: Aliens Onset.
In a seat, solemn,
ET's animal-nose
Emails a sonnet:
"Am I a stone lens?"

Male-ant noises.
I'm sanest alone
Online at a mass –

O silent as amen.
"I am a stone lens."

*

If we had friends, we'd think
fifty years without a word essential

If we had money
there 'd be days we'd blow the lot on party selves.

*

Over your little lives like the bodies of birds,
I called the winds of my love-and-art affairs
to scatter leaves, sweet leaves,
and apples and new handkerchiefs.

It was autumn though I didn't know it
because the wind smelled kind
and the dry leaves smelled of life,
and you weren't dead at all, but running, untouched,
towards your indestructible horizon.

I see you now for the last time, sentinel
in the iron branches over the iron bedstead
where I lie as I always lay,
solitary, naked, trying
to be covered by a wind of green kisses.

There could never have been a lover –
my love is not fitting.

Nor a child for my Poundland cradle –
my love is not fitting.

Nor a mother-and-father for my Judas kiss.
They had *True Love*. My love was never fitting.

But when I pray, is there nothing
unborn enough, unasking,

unseeing enough, enough
away to want no small-talk?

If it has heard of itself
it hears no news of our damage.

It is the *Unbeloved*:
the truth we have never failed,
who makest us also immeasurable.

Who art within our syndrome.

Fiona Sampson

Albania

What do they talk about
kicking off their flip-flops
spreading out carrier bags
father and son who pass
a round loaf to and fro
and face the coast our ferry
works along for hours
steady as going on foot
yes they seem to say
we know about going
on foot we have learnt
steadiness in lives
not much visited
by wonder working lives
which sacrifice us yet
do not extinguish us
here we are carried
over the shining sea
and just like in stories
our beautiful women
are waiting just one day
away just one more day.

Ian Seed

Russian Bar in Turin

It's a place I have just stumbled upon, yet I've been living here for years. I order a red-coloured drink whose name I mispronounce. The barman sniggers. In a corner, a big Russian man is holding forth to some Italians. In Russia, he says, under communism, at least everyone had a job. The Italians nod like children. It's then that I notice the red flag with hammer and sickle on the wall behind him. Speaking of the necessity of every individual joining the Revolution, the Russian flips a beer mat into the air, and gestures for me to catch it. The Italians watch me expectantly.

Jo Shapcott

At Guy's Hospital

Come in, come in
my name is Doctor Keats,
I'm glad you found your way
safely to the Southwark Wing,
Blue Zone, because the online
map can seem a bit
fevered to the poorly,
the way it swipes and zooms
under your finger-trembles.

Sit down: you are pale, your pulse
is fretful and when I ask you what
you see when your eyes are
closed I want you to tell me
about the pink wall of your eyelids
the veins and tendrils and floaters
not night-time in an English wood
thick with such life your ears and nose
send purple, sunburn and thickets
to fill your brain with Old Nature
only a shadow-knowledge to us now.

You ask me about your prognosis
because I can see inside your body:
I have built for you a magnetic resonance
imaging machine and will thread
you through it, open you out
in sequences, all your soft artifacts
and concurrent planes pouring into
the screen. You will cease. That much
is clear. If I were you I would stay
melodious for as long as you've got,
blushful and ready to be shaken, always,
by your first love, your first sleep.

Peter Sirr

Riff for Beatriz

Ab joi et ab joven m'apais

I feed on joy and youth   the rest
forget   all texts
abandoned   I feed
with joy   I feed on on you or would
were you here   were I there
by the lake   in the wood   where the
nightingales are   I hear them
the buds along the branches roar
the frost withdraw   I feast on the season
that you may come to me
like light to the trees   I set
my pilgrim heart to roam
I am here   your loosened armour   your
Saracen hands   I feed
on spices and desert air
the rest is argument   discourse
the lines unwinding
the lines bound like the twigs of a broom
to sweep you away and pull you back
my dust is yours together we blow through the meadows
I was here but now
a stir of language in the trees   birdsong
in the composed season   a voice
before the frost comes   before the wind and the rains
bear me off   come to me please

(PS, mostly)

Di Slaney

Doubtful words

She says it's a long love that has no turning.
She says basic rations are health and happiness,
and in case of doubtful words we must trust our
stock of defence bonds, tally the beasts for market
and spread the year's quota of muck over the fields
before Lady Day rent falls due. She says I should
know what it is, that Dad left me this, the papers
browned by his sweat, fingered by hope and
disaster, counting down days till the hay is all
gathered and the land has been mown. Then we lie
fallow, cut off by the dark with nights slamming
like sashes, saving our tallow for Midwinter Eve,
the rut that restocks us, God willing, she says.

Jos Smith

A Whole Herd of Bodies with Round Lashed Eyes

Imagine a poem for the Friesians on Cadbury Hill.
A giant, nervous poem with a growling belly
that stands uneasily upright on the page, waiting
for the reader to move along, move along, go.

A poem that carries its vowels in canvas stretchers,
staggering perhaps, grave and over-emotional,
full of hormones not all its own; easily startled.
A cow like these would appreciate a soft poem.

Wide stanzas that lean on one another
and breathe back and forth with cavernous lungs
and wonder about the shape of the moon at night.
The moon who always knows what a cow is thinking.

A poem that begins the way only the meek can lead
but drags behind it the whole of human language
clattering like pots and pans in the swimming mist. Cow-curiosity,
muscling forward when the reader's back is turned.

A slow and searching inquiry, like a whole herd of bodies
with round, lashed eyes, expectantly waiting
for the answer to a question that you might have missed,
that perhaps even they have misheard.

Imagine a poem for the Friesians on Cadbury Hill.
A poem that offers its wet nose up,
muddling its soul through bloodshot eyes,
balancing passions mysterious, even to itself.

Julian Stannard

Stations of the Cross

Someone had taken an axe
to my life which meant
that although everything
was in pieces we needed
a Christmas tree
if only for the children
to gather round as they listened
to a wound-up version of
Stille Nacht, Heilige Nacht.

Someone had taken an axe
to the forest – now there were
Christmas trees throughout the city.
Lucky me! I took myself
to the Mercato Orientale
to pick up my tree
and screw down the thorns
because someone had
taken an axe to my life.

I picked up my Christmas tree
and carried it all the way
to our house on the hill
which had turned into
an outpost of hell but
even hell wants a Christmas tree
UN ALBERO DI NATALE.

I carried my tree
past the Hotel Metropoli
I carried my tree
to Saint Anna's Funicular.
Oh, they said,

it's St Julian the leper
Julian of the *mot juste*
Julian with an axe in his head
carrying a Christmas tree
to an outpost of hell.

Sometimes people swung
a punch
just for the hell of it.
Someone started hammering
a nail into my head
just for the hell of it.
Evidently
I had done something wrong!
Then I carried my tree along
Corso Magenta where the blind man
turned a blind eye.

And I carried my tree
up Salita Santa Maria della Sanità
and I carried my tree to the eighth floor
because the lift was broken
and the woman who'd taken an axe
to my life said, Ah, un albero di natale,
we've been waiting so fucking long
for un albero di natale.

Put it there in the corner.
Careful, careful.
Oh look it's beautiful,
a little red perhaps
but beautiful. Here's a cloth
to wipe your face.
You'll frighten the children.
They'll think you've gone mad.

Em Strang

Bird-Woman

> 'Nothing is yet in its true form'
> CS Lewis

The bird-woman is in the field in her blue dress,
small bird wrapped in a rag of cotton in her hand,
legs like twigs, throat between songs.

The sunlight is squeezing her, squeezing the field-grass
until her blue dress is a distant boat
and the field is the sea,
somewhere used to slipping boundaries.

Then two men, hands in pockets,
feet sinking into the grey-black of the road.
The sun is hot and high and they wade into the field,
lose themselves to the waist in straight, green blades.

The bird-woman is scuffing the soft, loose earth,
making a bowl for the body.
She lays the bird with its broken neck
and covers it with clover,
small red flowers, lucky leaves.

When the men capsize her
the pleats of her dress unfurl.

The ground takes their weight.

Katharine Towers

rain

if we stand in woods after rain when the trees are iron and purple, like wine, we'll wish we could stay – not to wait for the woollen comfort of dusk, nor to hear the wind flinching back from the heart to let it be quiet and still...but to stand in the iron and purple of evening, our stories behind us like toys we've forgotten or lost, till we enter at last that place in the heart (that place in the dark of the heart) where there's nothing, not even weather

RA Villanueva

Saudade

Yes now, like you, I wonder: where
is the patron saint of exiles
and far districts, this prefecture
of salt licks, pollen? Of alleys

blue with plaques? And who among those
martyrs gives the nieces we have
yet to hold close our faces to
learn, our names to try? Who will halve

our pills for us, heat the bacon
fat, steep the tea? Everywhere wine
and moss. Everywhere fog. *The wrecks
of ships around the Whitefish Point*

*and bodies the lake won't give back,
you say: like that – a love like that.*

Mark Waldron

No More Mr Nice Guy

This then,
what you actually witness here, before your
very eyelids, is an actual blooming waste of time, in action,

in real time. I squid you not, certain shall we say 'people'
with a certain shall we say 'cheek' have had a go at me about
punctuality & punctuation, specifically the use

or otherwise of ampersands & obscenities and rubbish
and whatnot. As well as my peculiar drinking and poking fun
at people with or without disabilities and so on.

Well from now on, from the very next thing I do onwards,
I'm going to do exactly as I blinking well please, which is to be
marvellously wretched & frightened and broken and hidden.

Julia Webb

Sisters (part i)

(1)

This sister is the bones of the outfit,
she is the stuff that keeps the body up,
she is *dem bones, dem bones,*
she is calcified connective tissue,
she is femur, tibia, ulna, ribs.

(2)

This sister is the perfect scrunch
of English Rose,
all delicate petal curl, subtle pinks,
she opens her smile up to the sun.
This sister is a fuzzy stamen
with a dust of pollen,
she is the heady waft of perfume
begging you to bring your face down to her,
to bring your face right down.

(3)

She is the one with the hair just-so,
the handkerchief skirt hems, the well cut clothes,
and on birthdays she gets the family all together –
we line up for photos that never looked posed,
and how she laughs at being vegetarian
but each Christmas allowing herself a little meat.

She is the one with the dainty features, the cutesy nose,
the one they look for when you enter the room,

and the way they hang on her words makes you nauseous
but you can't say it, because she was the one
who watched out for you behind the shops and in the playground.

She is the one with the amicable divorce
and the books on cake decorating –
all those fiddly womanly things you have no patience for,
and she is the one who sat up all night in the crematorium
plaiting flowers into your mother's hair.

(4)

This sister reads Nietzsche,
her hair is twisted into bunches like tiny horns,
she makes abstract art with fur and feathers,
she likes to collect things from gutters and pavements,
and her eyes have that sparkle you were scared of as a kid.

(5)

This sister is the bee
and we are the nectar,

she is drawing us in
with her persistent buzzing,

her talk of the hive mind,
her tremble dance.

Grace Wells

Otter

Some things happened that should not have,
I made mistakes and was given witness to my worst self—

I was left like something a spider leaves,
sucked of everything except despair.

We founder and must find ways to mend.
One foot in front of the other I walked the riverbank,

inland, upstream, letting water flow against my failings.
I struck a path through cow-parsley and nettle,

holding the indigo lamp of bluebells to my damage,
moving deeper toward the river's quiet country,

further into my personal ruin. Where the two
converged I slumped among the wet weeds, wanting

the river to wash right through me, to wipe me clean.
And up from the liquid surface rose an otter;

an otter plunging the water. It dived to somersault,
to divide in two and become a mated pair.

Black as eels but halo-bright they circled, swimming
me into their carnival, into a wider world—

so that I want to say, do not fear your anguish;
despair births miracles; hope is only waiting for release.

Pay attention, the signs gifted are subtle: small beads
for the necklace of faith we must thread for ourselves.

Sarah Westcott

Inklings

Sometimes when we make love near the window
I can almost feel them waiting in the corners,
whispering in dusty spaces above the wardrobe,
their breath in drifts of light across the glaucous room,
and sometimes I glimpse filaments brushing against the panes,
delicate as spider silk – sense shifts in matter, stirrings,
and then it doesn't take much to bring them into our warm bed,
to call them down, the two of us moving together,
moulding them out of our hearts like clay,
with the mortar and pestle of our bodies,
the cups and planes of our hips
and thighbones working like engines all greased with blood and longing,
for soon we are reaching towards shining crowns,
our fingers straining to touch them,
and breathing out in one long rush into their starry lungs,
and sometimes afterwards if we are still they might come into focus,
step forward into the light, already entirely themselves.

Anna Wigley

Bryony's Visit

You arrived like the past I wished for:
all shy confidence,
all legs and hair.

You made of your room a teenager's lair:
all mirrors propped,
all flimsy clothes dropped.

You lived on coffee and air:
your lips the sacred
portals, guarded with care.

You were always late, appearing
at the very last moment
on the stair

with your hair sleek and straight;
looking like a race horse
ready at the gate.

Luke Wright

To London...

To London then, that fatted beast
on which the whole world comes to feast,
all private woe and public farce;
where money twerks its oiled arse
in gorgeous, fenced-off Georgian squares
and starchy oligarchical lairs;
where soaring, steel-glass towers sit
in ancient, ghoulish, plague-filled pits;
where gap-toothed roads left by the Blitz
are soaked in years of pigeon shit;
where listless folk roam airless malls
as slaves to airbrushed siren calls
then, gobsmacked, flash their plastic cash
and fill their hearts and lungs with ash;
where policy is signed and sealed
then forced upon the shires and fields;
where money men spin even more
from love of it and fear of war
(like bookie blokes they will their stocks
as food bank queues ring grotty blocks);
where cut-glass vowels meet glottal stops;
where half-cut kids in chicken shops
dream dreams as false as talent shows,
these rebels wrapped in branded clothes,
this lunar race illuminated
by their screens but never sated,
all within their reach at last
but safe behind the steel-laced glass –
it's oh so close but out of touch,
it's not for you, they know that much,
it's not for you, it's not for you,
it's not for you...
                    to London then.

Biographies of the shortlisted writers

Forward Prize for Best Collection

Vahni Capildeo (b. 1973 Port of Spain, Trinidad) writes that, throughout her childhood, 'my mother recited poetry by heart in French, various Caribbean dialects, and English, for the love of it, as did my father in Hindi and English'. Capildeo's own poetry is characterised by a kind of omnivorous, long-armed reach. Many-tongued and multi-cultural, her work sweeps through long prose poems and short imagistic bursts, through surrealism and gritty realism, acutely seeking the right form for each individual thought.

Capildeo has lived in the UK since 1991, studying Old Norse at Christ Church, Oxford, and working as an etymologist on the Oxford English Dictionary. She is able to summon double – or triple – perspectives on the questions of colonialism, migration and expatriation, which she explores as ruthlessly as she explores questions of the stability and fitness of language. Her work is infused with 'the sense of coexistent distance-in-presence, presence-in-distance', which she characterises as typical of electronic communication today, while showing 'how travellers carry elsewhen as well as elsewhere in their heart'.

Ian Duhig (b. 1954 London) is particularly celebrated for his poem 'The Lammas Hireling', which won both the National Poetry Competition and the 2001 Forward Prize for Best Single Poem. Having worked with homeless people for 15 years and finding, as he writes, that 'location and poetry dissolve into each other for me', Duhig has inserted a rare depth of understanding of his native Leeds into his poetry.

'Poetry drew me in because it can contain so much so easily in its own paradoxical compass,' he has written. Certainly paradoxical clashes frequently find expression in his poetry: modern chatter alongside myth and lore; litheness of thought alongside strict metrical forms; a mischievous humour alongside a devastating sense of tragedy. Chosen as one of the Poetry Book Society's New Generation Poets in 1994 along with Carol Ann Duffy and Simon Armitage, Duhig shares those poets' ability to dramatise contemporary concerns in technically accomplished verse.

Duhig's advice to aspiring poets is practical: 'Learn to live on very little. Never underestimate what a massive pain in the arse you will be to your loved ones and everybody else. Be lucky and be kind.'

Choman Hardi (b. 1974 Sulaimani, Iraq) came to the UK as an asylum seeker and has degrees from Oxford, UCL and Kent. As a Kurdish poet, born in Iraqi Kurdistan, and raised in a repressive, patriarchal society, she writes poems about, arising from, or in response to the intersecting inequalities she has seen. This is the subject she continues to research as an assistant professor in the department of English in the American University of Iraq, Sulaimani.

Hardi's family fled to Iran when she was 14, and it was then, learning Persian and reading the modern Persian poets, that Hardi first came to poetry. She began writing poems soon after, inspired by love, 'real, tangible, and tidal'.

As well as two collections in Kurdish, Hardi has published one previous collection in English, *Life for Us*. Bernard O'Donoghue wrote that he had 'rarely read a book which so indisputably establishes the capacity of poetry to express the historical and political'. In response to her Forward shortlisting, Hardi writes that she can now believe that those she 'tried to give voice to in *Considering the Women* will be heard, that bearing witness is valued, that telling the truth about the human condition is necessary'.

Alice Oswald (b. 1966 Reading), Devon-based gardener and classicist, is as a poet intricately engaged with nature, and with histories both communal and linguistic. Her second book, *Dart*, published in 2002, trailed the river Dart from its source, through the communities which rely on its waters, down to its mouth.

Since receiving the TS Eliot Prize for that collection, her reputation has grown; her subsequent books – including *Woods etc.* and *Memorial* – have received the Geoffrey Faber Memorial Prize, the Hawthornden Prize and the Ted Hughes Award, among many others.

Oswald recalls that she began writing poetry at age eight when, after a sleepless night, she found herself 'astonished by the clouds at dawn and realised they required a different kind of language'. This search for a different kind of language runs through her career; her subjects –

whether water, flowers, insects or Agamemnon – never settle down or still, are never simply their present selves.

Falling Awake – which includes 'Dunt', the 2007 winner of the Forward Prize for Best Single Poem – aims, writes Oswald, 'to speak relentlessly, anonymously, almost inadvertently, (as insects do) without using the mouth'.

Denise Riley (b. 1948 Carlisle) is a philosopher and feminist theorist as well as a poet. She's written eight works of non-fiction, including *'Am I That Name?': Feminism and the Category of 'Women' in History*.

Riley can be seen as the UK's best answer to the New York School poets, a movement whose riotous running together of art theory and philosophy with everyday speech and pop culture has been one of the dominant trends in poetry over the last half-century. From her first book, *Marxism for Infants*, through to her astonishingly varied and ambitious *Mop Mop Georgette*, she has successfully sought to make abstract intellectual questions vivid, pressing and personal.

In *Say Something Back*, Riley explores how our personal concerns – loss, cruelty, mortality – have implications for the way in which we, as a species, exist within the world. Central to the book is her elegy 'A Part Song' – winner of the 2012 Forward Prize for Best Single Poem – which was written after the death of her son. She says it was composed 'in imagined solidarity with the endless others whose adult children have died, often in far worse circumstances'.

Forward Prize for Best First Collection

Nancy Campbell (b. 1978 Exeter) grew up in Berwickshire, Scotland. She began writing *Disko Bay* while writer-in-residence in the world's most northerly museum, on the island of Upernavik, at the same time as her abecedarium *How To Say I Love You In Greenlandic: An Arctic Alphabet* (winner of the Birgit Skiöld Award). She suggests that 'the darkness of the polar winter may come across in the tone of the collection'. Campbell's book also 'considers the connections between northern Europe and the Arctic, looking at migrations across the North Sea and the Greenland Sea, as well as the consequences of colonialism and climate change'.

Campbell trained originally as a printmaker and is currently editor of *Printmaking Today*, a position that focuses her interest on 'the material form that has for so long been a central concern of my work'. A delicate understanding of balance – ecological, social and visual – underwrites her work as poet.

Ron Carey (b. 1948 Limerick) has been a winner or finalist in a host of poetry competitions: the Bridport Prize, Lightship International Poetry Prize, Cinnamon Press Poetry Awards, Fish International Poetry Prize, Gregory O'Donoghue International Poetry Awards, Hugh O'Flaherty Poetry Award, iYeats Poetry Competition and the Wasafiri New Writing Prize for Poetry – the list goes on.

He says 'there was a tradition of storytelling and reciting in the family and in the community' which contributed to his genesis as a writer. The poems in *Distance* are, he writes, 'centred on relationships between people in Time and Space'.

After a working life that started with cutting and drilling steel, Carey took up poetry seriously in his sixties and received an MA in creative writing in 2015. He reminds younger poets that 'a poet does not have to come fully formed out of the workshop'. Indeed, it is the relationship between ourselves and the world, Carey's work implies, that produces the meaningful stuff of poetry.

Harry Giles (b. 1986 Walthamstow) grew up in Orkney. He trained as a theatre director, but has supported himself creating computer games: both professions feed into his dramatic, often playful, poetry. He says, 'My writing is still rooted in that interest in orality and aurality and in meeting an audience.' Since winning the BBC Slam championship in 2009, he frequently writes and performs his verse in a 'magpie' version of Scots, a development which has allowed him to begin 'to express parts of myself that had been hidden away'.

The decision to write in Scots, which is 'one movement in this problem of how to keep alive linguistic diversity in the era of globalised English', indicates Giles' commitment to radical politics. This is also a hallmark of his previous publications – including *Oam*, a 2013 pamphlet written as part of a residency at Govanhill baths in Glasgow, from which 'The Hairdest Man in Govanhill' is taken.

It is with *Tonguit*, then, that Giles has begun to move outwards from that position. 'I had a lot of questions about my identity, my home, my language, my struggle with belonging,' he says, 'and by the end of the book I felt like I had enough answers to do something new.'

Ruby Robinson (b. 1985 Manchester) grew up in Sheffield and Doncaster; her poetry has been published in *The Poetry Review* and *Poetry* magazine. She draws inspiration from writing which takes her 'somewhere unexpected', and lists previous Forward Prize-winners Ted Hughes and Claudia Rankine as among those who have left a lasting impression on her.

Robinson says that, as a child, she used to 'write things down that angered or confused me, in lieu of being able to protest out loud'. This relationship between sound, quietness and expression is an important part of *Every Little Sound*, with its epigraph from tinnitus expert Dr David Baguley: 'Internal gain – an internal volume control which helps us amplify and focus upon quiet sounds in times of threat, danger or intense concentration.' Robinson brings that intense concentration to the otherwise drowned-out sounds of our everyday internal world.

Tiphanie Yanique (b. 1978 St Thomas, Virgin Islands) has long considered herself a writer; indeed, when asked in school for three words to describe herself, she would say, 'Caribbean, girl, writer'. Further, she notes how children 'speak in metaphor, that they hunt down language as poets do, that they use their vocabulary limitations the way poets might use the limitations of poetic form – to find a way to say something anew'.

Wife was begun in 2000, but became increasingly focused: the more recently written poems 'are more clearly about the complexities of heterosexual marriage'. It has already won the 2016 Bocas Poetry Prize.

Yanique, who was taught by Claudia Rankine, winner of the 2015 Forward Prize, says of teachers that they 'can destroy you or they can build you. Sometimes they do one in service of the other'.

Asked what is next for her as a poet, Yanique replies, 'I have a lingering feeling that there is more I might be able to discover about the ways in which being a woman inside of a family and being an island inside of a nation are connected.'

Forward Prize for Best Single Poem

Sasha Dugdale (b. 1974 Sussex) is renowned as a translator of poetry, and has published numerous books of poetry and plays translated from Russian, as well as three collections of her own poetry – most recently *Red House*. As editor of the acclaimed magazine *Modern Poetry in Translation*, she is immersed in world poetry, and writes that 'I read this work because I need to – it is like a vitamin injection. English suddenly seems bigger and richer and I itch to write again.'

Dugdale recognises that writing can be a matter of 'tending' a poem, and notes that 'tending poetry is still harder for women, who are often juggling jobs and being carers'. This observation gives resonance to the poignant line in her shortlisted poem 'Joy', in which Catherine Blake – the recent widow of William – speaks the words 'I tend the light'. In this very long poem of affection and loss, Dugdale carefully conjures 'the natural grief of losing a life-partner', while weighing 'what it would be like to lose a partner in creativity, in poetry'.

Rachel Hadas (b. 1948 New York, USA) is an American poet, prose-writer and translator, who is currently professor of English at Rutgers University, in Newark, New Jersey.

Hadas describes her project as being one of 'negotiating the divide between inside (memories, emotions, dreams) and outside (the weather of the world)'. It is the ability to span this fraught distance that marks out her work, and 'Roosevelt Hospital Blues' is no exception. The poem gets its electricity from the contrast between, on the one hand, its thumping, blues-format rhymes and repetitions and, on the other, the sheer variety and amount of ground it manages to cover. Stark considerations of mortality rub up against American slang and love-song sentiment.

Hadas's most recent book of poems is *Questions in the Vestibule*. Asked what's next, Hadas notes that she has an 'immense pile of uncollected poems that is beginning to pluck at me and ask for some overdue attention, the way my elderly cat does'.

David Harsent (b. 1942 Devon) is the author of 11 collections of poetry, that have between them accumulated a wide array of prizes, from *Legion*'s Forward Prize for Best Collection, to *Night*'s Griffin International

Poetry Prize, to *Fire Songs'* 2014 TS Eliot Prize. He is currently a professor of creative writing at the University of Roehampton.

Harsent describes *Salt* as 'a group of short poems that have a common tone and mood', and it is this mood that is particularly valuable in the work. Robert Frost talks about the 'sound of sense' but Harsent excels at something further – a kind of 'sound of significance'; a subtle, careful music which urges the reader towards a deeper-than-usual meditation. Music, indeed, is another important aspect of Harsent's practice. He has collaborated with a number of composers, most significantly with Harrison Birtwistle, on several widely performed works.

Harsent has recently published a book of versions of poems by the Greek poet Yannis Ritsos, and the works in *Salt* – with their muted, uncertain backgrounds offering up sudden vivid flashes of colour and significance – evoke something of those Ritsos poems.

Melissa Lee-Houghton (b. 1982 Manchester) publishes her third collection, *Sunshine*, in September 2016, following a book of essays, *An Insight Into Mental Health in Britain*. She was selected as one of the Next Generation Poets by the Poetry Book Society in 2014.

Lee-Houghton says she sensed as a child that contemporary poetry went 'against all the ideas I was being taught that as a human being we must be sensible, limited, in control of our feelings'. Something of this remains in her impetus to speak out against stifling consensus, and she describes writing 'i am very precious' partly as a way to 'express my outrage at the continued oppression I experience as a woman who both enjoys and fears sex'.

Her shortlisted poem features passages of rough acceleration and dizzying handbrake turns. The energy of the poem's sex-and-death abandonment drives it through its range of scenarios, fantasies, terrors, political broadsides, confessions, self-confrontations and redemptions. It is a work that meets face-to-face the subjects it insists cannot be separated cleanly: pornography, mental health, sexual desire, misogyny, maternity, pleasure and loss.

Solmaz Sharif (b. 1983 Istanbul, Turkey) studied at the University of California, Berkeley, and New York University. She has received numerous awards and fellowships, including a 'Discovery'/*Boston Review*

Poetry Prize, and is a former managing director of the Asian American Writers' Workshop.

Sharif, whose parents were both Iranian, writes that she admires most those poets 'who refuse to bar the political from their work while refusing to capitulate to it'. This balancing act is recognisable in 'Force Visibility', her shortlisted poem. As she describes it, the poem 'deals with the language of state-sponsored violence. Or the violence of state-sponsored language', noting that 'the words that appear in small caps are terms taken from the U.S. Department of Defense's Dictionary of Military and Associated Terms'. What's striking about the poem, though, in its almost queasy intrusion of the public and the private worlds into one another, is the disorienting effect of its overlaid perspectives, the impression of several lives being lived at once.

Publisher acknowledgements

Emily Blewitt · This Is Not a Rescue · *And Other Poems*
Nancy Campbell · Malinguartoq / The dance ·
   The hunter's wife becomes the sun · *Disko Bay* · Enitharmon Press
Vahni Capildeo · Investigation of Past Shoes · Stalker ·
   Measures of Expatriation · Carcanet
Ron Carey · Upstairs · The Murderer's Dog · *Distance* · Revival Press
John Clegg · Socorro · *Holy Toledo!* · Carcanet
Phillip Crymble · Onions · *Not Even Laughter* · Salmon Poetry
Kate Dempsey · While It Lasted · *The Space Between* · Doire Press
Edward Doegar · Underground · *The Rialto*
Maura Dooley · In a dream she meets him again · *The Silvering* ·
   Bloodaxe Books
Sasha Dugdale · *from* Joy · *PN Review*
Ian Duhig · Blockbusters · Bridled Vows · *The Blind Roadmaker* ·
   Picador Poetry
Will Eaves · The appeal of automation… · *The Inevitable Gift Shop* ·
   CB editions
Andy Fletcher · the atlas · *How To Be A Bomb* · Wrecking Ball Press
Leontia Flynn · The Radio · *Poetry Ireland Review*
Linda France · Adaptation · *Reading the Flowers* · Arc Publications
Tom French · A Music Room · *The Way to Work* · The Gallery Press
Harry Giles · Brave · The Hairdest Man in Govanhill · *Tonguit* ·
   Freight Books
Rachel Hadas · Roosevelt Hospital Blues · *Times Literary Supplement*
Choman Hardi · Dispute Over a Mass Grave · Researcher's Blues ·
   Considering the Women · Bloodaxe Books
David Harsent · *from* Salt · *Poetry London*
Tracey Herd · The Imaginary Death of Star · *Not in This World* ·
   Bloodaxe Books
Sarah Howe · Pronouns are for slackers · Clinic Press
Kathleen Jamie · Blossom · *The Bonniest Companie* · Picador Poetry
Luke Kennard · Enter Cain · *Cain* · Penned in the Margins
Kate Kilalea · Sometimes I think the world is just a vast breeding ground
   for mosquitoes · *Tender Journal*

Peter Knaggs · Badger the Cadger · *You're so vain, you probably think this book is about you* · Wrecking Ball Press

Melissa Lee-Houghton · i am very precious · *Prac Crit*

Angela Leighton · Roundel for the Children · *Spills* · Carcanet

William Letford · This is it · *Dirt* · Carcanet

Fran Lock · Melpomene · *The Poetry Review*

Hannah Lowe · Gloves · *Chan* · Bloodaxe Books

Kathryn Maris · It was discovered that gut bacteria were responsible · *Granta*

Cathal McCabe · Snow · *Outer Space: Selected Poems* · Metre Editions

Roy McFarlane · Papers · *Beginning With Your Last Breath* · Nine Arches Press

JO Morgan · There was her... · *Interference Pattern* · Cape Poetry

Helen Mort · Mountain · *No Map Could Show Them* · Chatto & Windus

Andrew Motion · Felling a Tree · *Peace Talks* · Faber & Faber

Karthika Nair · Bedtime Story for a Dasi's Son · *Until the Lions* · Arc Publications

Katrina Naomi · The Bicycle · *The Way the Crocodile Taught Me* · Seren

Sharon Olds · Sheffield Mountain Ode · *Odes* · Cape Poetry

Alice Oswald · Flies · Slowed-Down Blackbird · *Falling Awake* · Cape Poetry

Nigel Pantling · Striking the Deal · *Kingdom Power Glory* · smith | doorstop books

Denise Riley · Listening for lost people · The patient who had no insides · *Say Something Back* · Picador Poetry

Ruby Robinson · Undress · Apology · *Every Little Sound* · Part of the Pavilion Poetry series (published by Liverpool University Press)

Amali Rodrigo · Satī · *The Lotus Gatherers* · Bloodaxe Books

Michael Rosen · Dustman · *Don't Mention the Children* · Smokestack Books

Carol Rumens · On the Spectrum · *Animal People* · Seren

Fiona Sampson · Albania · *The Catch* · Chatto & Windus

Ian Seed · Russian Bar in Turin · *Identity Papers* · Shearsman Books

Jo Shapcott · At Guy's Hospital · *Southword Journal Online*

Solmaz Sharif · Force Visibility · *Granta*

Peter Sirr · Riff for Beatriz · *Sway* · The Gallery Press

Di Slaney · Doubtful words · *Reward for Winter* · Valley Press

Jos Smith · A Whole Herd of Bodies with Round Lashed Eyes ·
  Subterranea · Arc Publications
Julian Stannard · Stations of the Cross · *What were you thinking?* ·
  CB editions
Em Strang · Bird-Woman · *Bird-Woman* · Shearsman Books
Katharine Towers · rain · *The Remedies* · Picador Poetry
RA Villanueva · Saudade · *Prac Crit*
Mark Waldron · No More Mr Nice Guy · *Meanwhile, Trees* ·
  Bloodaxe Books
Julia Webb · Sisters (part i) · *Bird Sisters* · Nine Arches Press
Grace Wells · Otter · *Fur* · Dedalus Press
Sarah Westcott · Inklings · *Slant Light* · Part of the Pavilion Poetry series
  (published by Liverpool University Press)
Anna Wigley · Bryony's Visit · *Ghosts* · Gomer Press
Luke Wright · To London… · *What I Learned from Johnny Bevan* ·
  Penned in the Margins
Tiphanie Yanique · Zuihitsu for the day I cheat on my husband,
  to my fiancé · Altar Call · *Wife* · Peepal Tree Press

Winners of the Forward Prizes

Best Collection

2015 · Claudia Rankine · *Citizen: An American Lyric* · Penguin Books

2014 · Kei Miller · *The Cartographer Tries to Map a Way to Zion* · Carcanet

2013 · Michael Symmons Roberts · *Drysalter* · Cape Poetry

2012 · Jorie Graham · *PLACE* · Carcanet

2011 · John Burnside · *Black Cat Bone* · Cape Poetry

2010 · Seamus Heaney · *Human Chain* · Faber & Faber

2009 · Don Paterson · *Rain* · Faber & Faber

2008 · Mick Imlah · *The Lost Leader* · Faber & Faber

2007 · Sean O'Brien · *The Drowned Book* · Picador Poetry

2006 · Robin Robertson · *Swithering* · Picador Poetry

2005 · David Harsent · *Legion* · Faber & Faber

2004 · Kathleen Jamie · *The Tree House* · Picador Poetry

2003 · Ciaran Carson · *Breaking News* · The Gallery Press

2002 · Peter Porter · *Max is Missing* · Picador Poetry

2001 · Sean O'Brien · *Downriver* · Picador Poetry

2000 · Michael Donaghy · *Conjure* · Picador Poetry

1999 · Jo Shapcott · *My Life Asleep* · OUP

1998 · Ted Hughes · *Birthday Letters* · Faber & Faber

1997 · Jamie McKendrick · *The Marble Fly* · OUP

1996 · John Fuller · *Stones and Fires* · Chatto & Windus

1995 · Sean O'Brien · *Ghost Train* · OUP

1994 · Alan Jenkins · *Harm* · Chatto & Windus

1993 · Carol Ann Duffy · *Mean Time* · Anvil Press

1992 · Thom Gunn · *The Man with Night Sweats* · Faber & Faber

Best First Collection

2015 · Mona Arshi · *Small Hands* · Liverpool University Press

2014 · Liz Berry · *Black Country* · Chatto & Windus

2013 · Emily Berry · *Dear Boy* · Faber & Faber

2012 · Sam Riviere · *81 Austerities* · Faber & Faber

2011 · Rachael Boast · *Sidereal* · Picador Poetry

2010 · Hilary Menos · *Berg* · Seren

2009 · Emma Jones · *The Striped World* · Faber & Faber

2008 · Kathryn Simmonds · *Sunday at the Skin Launderette* · Seren

2007 · Daljit Nagra · *Look We Have Coming to Dover!* · Faber & Faber

2006 · Tishani Doshi · *Countries of the Body* · Aark Arts

2005 · Helen Farish · *Intimates* · Cape Poetry

2004 · Leontia Flynn · *These Days* · Cape Poetry

2003 · AB Jackson · *Fire Stations* · Anvil Press

2002 · Tom French · *Touching the Bones* · The Gallery Press

2001 · John Stammers · *Panoramic Lounge-Bar* · Picador Poetry

2000 · Andrew Waterhouse · *In* · The Rialto

1999 · Nick Drake · *The Man in the White Suit* · Bloodaxe Books

1998 · Paul Farley · *The Boy from the Chemist is Here to See You* · Picador Poetry

1997 · Robin Robertson · *A Painted Field* · Picador Poetry

1996 · Kate Clanchy · *Slattern* · Chatto & Windus

1995 · Jane Duran · *Breathe Now, Breathe* · Enitharmon

1994 · Kwame Dawes · *Progeny of Air* · Peepal Tree

1993 · Don Paterson · *Nil Nil* · Faber & Faber

1992 · Simon Armitage · *Kid* · Faber & Faber

Best Single Poem

2015 · Claire Harman · The Mighty Hudson · *Times Literary Supplement*

2014 · Stephen Santus · In a Restaurant · Bridport Prize

2013 · Nick MacKinnon · The Metric System · *The Warwick Review*

2012 · Denise Riley · A Part Song · *London Review of Books*

2011 · RF Langley · To a Nightingale · *London Review of Books*

2010 · Julia Copus · An Easy Passage · *Magma*

2009 · Robin Robertson · At Roane Head · *London Review of Books*

2008 · Don Paterson · Love Poem for Natalie "Tusja" Beridze · *The Poetry Review*

2007 · Alice Oswald · Dunt · *Poetry London*

2006 · Sean O'Brien · Fantasia on a Theme of James Wright · *The Poetry Review*

2005 · Paul Farley · Liverpool Disappears for a Billionth of a Second · *The North*

2004 · Daljit Nagra · Look We Have Coming to Dover! · *The Poetry Review*

2003 · Robert Minhinnick · The Fox in the Museum of Wales · *Poetry London*

2002 · Medbh McGuckian · She Is in the Past, She Has This Grace ·
  The Shop
2001 · Ian Duhig · The Lammas Hireling · National Poetry Competition
2000 · Tessa Biddington · The Death of Descartes · Bridport Prize
1999 · Robert Minhinnick · Twenty-five Laments for Iraq · *PN Review*
1998 · Sheenagh Pugh · Envying Owen Beattie · *New Welsh Review*
1997 · Lavinia Greenlaw · A World Where News Travelled Slowly ·
  Times Literary Supplement
1996 · Kathleen Jamie · The Graduates · *Times Literary Supplement*
1995 · Jenny Joseph · In Honour of Love · *The Rialto*
1994 · Iain Crichton Smith · Autumn · *PN Review*
1993 · Vicki Feaver · Judith · *Independent on Sunday*
1992 · Jackie Kay · Black Bottom · Bloodaxe Books

For more detail and further reading about the Forward Prizes, books and
associated programmes, see our website forwardartsfoundation.org or
follow us on Facebook or Twitter @forwardprizes